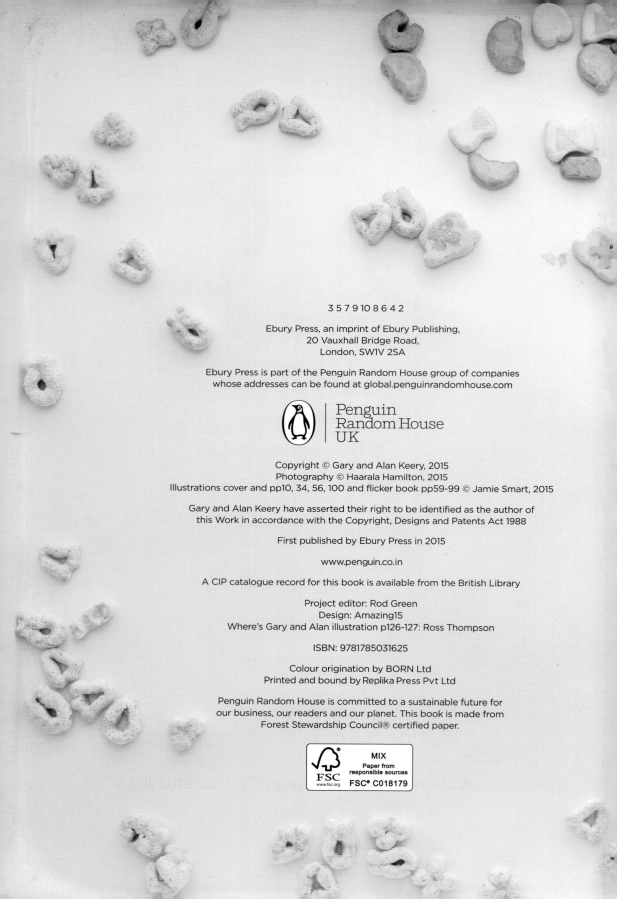

3 5 7 9 10 8 6 4 2

Ebury Press, an imprint of Ebury Publishing,
20 Vauxhall Bridge Road,
London, SW1V 2SA

Ebury Press is part of the Penguin Random House group of companies
whose addresses can be found at global.penguinrandomhouse.com

Penguin
Random House
UK

First published by Ebury Press in 2015

www.penguin.co.in

A CIP catalogue record for this book is available from the British Library

Project editor: Rod Green
Design: Amazing15
Where's Gary and Alan illustration p126-127: Ross Thompson

ISBN: 9781785031625

Colour origination by BORN Ltd
Printed and bound by Replika Press Pvt Ltd

Penguin Random House is committed to a sustainable future for
our business, our readers and our planet. This book is made from
Forest Stewardship Council® certified paper.

MIX
Paper from
responsible sources
FSC
www.fsc.org
FSC® C018179

CEREAL KILLER CAFE

COOKBOOK

A Bowlful of Recipes, Trivia and Fun

Alan and Gary Keery

STEP-1. S:25-3
m:3-3.7
L:3.5-4.4

2 FREE or 40p for PREMIUM

#3 +60 EACH

Pick Your CEREAL   CHOOSE YA MILK   Add Your TOPPINGS

RECIPES

GARY WOZ HERE!

GET IN Touch

/cerealkillercafe
/cerealkilleruk
@cerealkillercafe

FOUR
GRAB A DRINK

5 Treat Yo'self TO A OR **POPTART TOAST**

or choose a cereal cocktail!

FUN AND TRIVIA

INTRODU

Welcome to a book that will, hopefully, change how you view cooking ingredients, and get you to think outside of the (cereal) box.

In the early evening of Monday 10th May 1982, during an episode of Blue Peter, the sun was shining, and Kay and Herbie Keery were expecting two bouncing baby boys, Alan and Gary. The birth was without complications, although twins being born back in the 80s was quite a big deal apparently! Gary was born first with Herbie and two midwives in the room, nothing strange there, although when Alan started peeping his head out, the midwife swung the door open and shouted, 'The second twin is on its way!' The room then filled with doctors, nurses and students, and Alan entered the world to an audience of more than 20!

For the next 18 years there was a sibling rivalry between the pair that could only be matched by Bart and Lisa Simpson. Throughout adulthood the twins have remained side-by-side, and starting a business together was their next big step.

In today's world we are all so used to the same thing that when a new way of thinking happens, everyone can call you nuts! It wasn't long ago that someone put cheese-and-onion flavouring on popcorn, and everyone freaked out. And now a blue cheese, walnut and celery flavour actually exists, and no one bats an eyelid.

We questioned the norm and wanted to change how people view cereal by opening Europe's first café dedicated to selling it – and it's fair to say we divided opinions across the world. When the café opened we received marriage proposals, and death threats. We were visited on our opening day by Channel 4 News and accused of selling over-priced products in an underprivileged area of London. This caused a bit of a Channel 4 backlash, as many people translated the piece to 'Business Opens And Sells Products For More Than They Paid For Them' – a true shocker, I know!

At Cereal Killer Café we are selling more than just a bowl of cereal, we are selling a cereal experience. Our menu consists of 120 different cereals from around the world, with 78 different milks, and 20 toppings, meaning there are over one million different combinations you can create, all served up in a nostalgic café that transports people back to their childhood and reignites people with the love of cereal we all had as kids.

Our first memory of cereal is often our first memory of responsibility, being given the choice of choosing the cereal you would be eating every day for the next week was the most stressful thing you had to deal with as a kid... well, that and not pissing the bed or accidentally calling your teacher 'mummy' – the shame! Cereal is also the first meal we 'cooked' ourselves. Milk and cereal would always cover the kitchen counter, but geez, what an achievement. Soon after this we got to experience baking for the first time and a Rice Krispie cake or chocolate Cornflake bun was as far as our culinary skills would take us.

As we grew older a bowl of cereal after school would tide us over until we had our Findus Crispy Pancakes and chips. Cereal followed us into adulthood when facing the big bad world alone – it was the easiest and cheapest meal you could make. Cereal is more than a dry food covered in milk: it is a rite of passage, it can be our best friend and teacher, our crutch and our comforter. Cereal is everything.

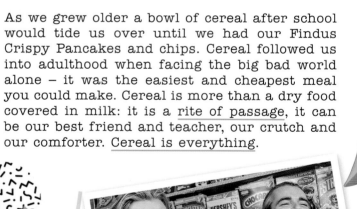

The idea for Cereal Killer Café was born when we were hungover one day (hangovers can induce the best and worst ideas) and fancied a bowl of cereal while out and about in Shoreditch, London. For many, cereal is a great hangover cure as it's not only a food but a drink too, and God knows you need fluids when you're hungover. However, we soon realised that you couldn't purchase cereal in cafés or restaurants in London, or even Europe for that matter! Our only option was to swing past Tesco and take a box back to our pokey flat above a kebab shop.

This seemed pretty nuts to us. How can a meal that is enjoyed by millions of people every day be restricted to being eaten at home? That's when the light-bulb moment came. If we opened a café that just sold cereal, we'd be tapping in to a massive gap in the market! And Cereal Killer Café was born.

The next year was filled with sourcing cereals and planning out every aspect of the business. We had a lot of feedback from friends and family, a lot of people thought we were mad and stupid to risk everything we had on such a crazy idea, and maybe we were, but I think all entrepreneurs will tell you, you have to have a little bit of crazy in you to start your own business.

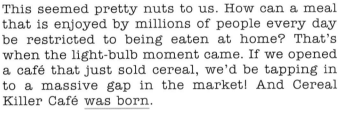

DRINKS
COCKTAILS

A FEW WORDS FROM BILLY...

Cereal is the best. Simply the best. So are cocktails. In this book there are five cocktails from me, Billy Rayner, a cocktail bartender with huge enthusiasm for twisting classic drinks and a deep love of cereal. I also have great admiration for what the Cereal Killer Café has done; which is to provide the person on the go with a quick bowl of awesome cereal.

These recipes are based on classics that are popular and would be great hits at parties — especially if you want to make a lasting impression on your guests. Cereals are so unique in their individual tastes and can completely substitute ANY drink's source of sugar content, giving it a whole new feel.

What I am saying is, hopefully this is the beginning of mass cereal cocktail revolution! Try it in anything — for instance, Cornflakes in or on top of your Bloody Mary. The thing is, if you have a favourite cereal, don't restrict it to the bowl and milk from which it came. If you have a favourite cocktail or any cocktail you have the time to try out at home, just muddle some of the cereal in the bottom of the glass, infuse for an hour with some liquor (aka, leave it in a bowl for a bit), stick it in a pan and make a syrup with it! The possibilities are endless.

The cocktails in this book are certainly not the craziest concoctions I could come up with using cereal (but beef-bouillon-infused fresh tobacco sprinkled with hickory-smoked Cap'n Crunch and blended with a Kentucky Rye whiskey with some blood orange juice is pretty crazy. But then, I am a freak), but they are great twists on classics. The last recipe is an original and will certainly not disappoint. More importantly, I hope these recipes act as triggers for all y'all to come up with even better drinks using our star ingredient: cereal. Cereals of the world unite!

BILLY
RAYNER

Cereal dust, aka condensed magic/dancing dust/devil's dandruff/sugar puff/frosted flakes, is a fine powder farmed in the southern region of cereal boxes in supermarket 'isles' across the country.

This powder has an addictive quality with some users prematurely gathering it using a colander. The effect on the user is a euphoric sugar high that is much greater than when the powder is consumed in its rock form: cereal.

We think this is the best possible use of your unwanted cereal dust. You can collect it over time and TBH it doesn't really matter which cereal dust it is, as the dusty powders of your combined favourite cereals will make this such a tasty treat. The amount of cereal you eat will determine how quickly you can collect the dust, although a speedy way to do it is to grab a colander and shake all your cereals around in it, collecting the dust on a large tray below.

2 SERVINGS
- 4 scoops vanilla ice cream
- 200ml whole milk
- 100g cereal dust

The only difficult part of this recipe is getting the cereal dust, really. So grab your blender and pop in the ice cream and the milk. Blend it all together until it has the consistency of, well, a milkshake. D'uh!

Now pour in the cereal dust and blitz it through the mixture. It's that easy. Now you have a cerealy sensation ready for drinking.

CEREAL DUST MILKSHAKE

CEREAL DUST

CEREAL
KILLER
MILK

We could raise a nationwide debate discussing whether or not to drink the milk left at the bottom of the cereal bowl. In the café it's pretty much a 50/50 split of the people slurping the sugared milk and those leaving it where it is.

And after much observing and character analysis, it is my conclusion that people who leave milk at the bottom of the bowl have sociopathic tendencies.

Drinking this milk is the perfect way to end the most amazing meal; it's like a final farewell from the sweet grains you've just ingested, and so therefore it should be worshipped. And this is why I bring you: Cereal Killer Milk. A lot of people will agree that the cerealy milk at the bottom of the bowl is the best part of breakfast, but sometimes you just don't get enough! Now let's show you how to make it in bulk...

2 SERVINGS
- 60g cereal of your choice (Frosties work like a dream)
- 1 pint milk of your choice (we prefer whole milk)

Toast the cereal under your grill on a low heat for 10 minutes, shaking halfway through or until slightly browned. Don't take your eyes off the wee flakes here, as you don't want them to burn!

Combine the toasted cereal with the milk in a jug or bowl and leave them to make friends with each other for an hour in the fridge.

Strain the chilled milk through a fine sieve, and press on the cereal to squeeze out as much liquid as possible.

Serve with a massive smile on your face!

This cocktail really will metaphorically punch you in the face; it's a strong rum-based cocktail which you should always remember to drink responsibly. And when I say drink responsibly, I mean always have a glass of water between drinks, identify a designated driver and pick your barf chunks out of the kitchen sink before going to bed.

Drinking a cocktail like this is something your teenage self would've sniggered at, as I'm sure, like most of our generation, your first night on the sauce started with your friend's older brother buying you a six-pack of hooch which you downed in a local park/forest/cemetery or wherever you got your kicks. And, like most of our generation, hilarity ensued. I will reluctantly tell you of my first experience.

A long story short, I was being driven home by my mum and I puked in the back of the car, but in my drunken state I used my open hand to block the vom from leaving my mouth, resulting in the vom spraying through my fingertips, and covering most of the interior of our Peugeot 106 and its passengers. Please don't judge me.

MAKES 1 DRINK

- 25ml peach brandy
- 20g Froot Loops
- 25ml dark rum (Captain Morgan or Kraken will do)
- 25ml brandy (Courvoisier or Martell will do)
- 10ml lemon juice
- 10ml lime juice
- Ice, ice baby
- Basil leaves, to decorate

Get a peach brandy or liqueur (a classic Archers peach schnapps will do, but come on, you're not at a hen party) and whack it in a saucepan on a medium heat with the Froot Loops. If you're using the British store-bought Froot Loops, add some sugar, but if you managed to get your hands on some American Froot Loops, then by golly they will be sweet enough.

Let it come to a boil for 10 seconds, then quickly take it off the heat and immediately drain the contents of the pan through a colander, just like pasta, catching the juices in a jug. Be careful not to let the liquid boil too fast as you don't want the alcohol to evaporate, otherwise you'll be drinking an alcohol-free cocktail – and we know they are only made for people without any friends.

(You'll probably want to nibble on the alcohol-soaked Froot Loops while you finish the concoction, and of course you should, they are now harnessing the magic of a tequila worm!)

Let the mixture cool for 15 minutes then pour the juices into that cocktail shaker at the back of your cupboard that you got for Christmas, and thought 'yeah, I'll use that all the time'. Add the rum, brandy, lemon and lime juice and ice, and shake it like you're getting paid for it.

Pour the cocktail into an old-fashioned tumbler – preferably over crushed ice, but cubed ice will do if you don't have crushed. Decorate with some sprigs of basil threaded through some fresh Froot Loops and – tah dah! Fruit Loop Punch.

FRUIT LOOP PUNCH

ICEBREAKER

We all love to be the life and soul of the party, but sometimes even those of us who find it difficult to stop talking for a second, even when we have been locked in a small, dark cupboard by our twin brother, can struggle a little to find something to say in polite company. To make sure that never happens to you, here is a list of cereal facts and myths to entertain your friends at parties.

Cornflakes were invented as part of an anti-masturbation crusade. John Harvey Kellogg was a Judeo-Christian, and thought sex was detrimental to physical health, and invented Cornflakes as a tool to help kids abstain from touching themselves.

Mother, Guess You'll Have to open the other Package of Kellogg's TOASTED CORN FLAKES
The Kind with the Flavor – Made from Selected White Corn
THE GENUINE ALWAYS HAS THIS SIGNATURE
W. K. Kellogg

Due to the addictive nature of carbohydrates, Special K cereal is more addictive than Special K the drug, aka ketamine.

Tony the Tiger is from a large Italian family, and his full name is Anthony the Tiger.

Rice Krispies don't make the Snap! Crackle! Pop! sound in every country.
Germany   Knisper! Knasper! Knusper!
Holland   Piff! Paff! Poff!
Finland   Riks! Raks! Poks!

Tony the Tiger has retired.

PARTY FACTS

In 1972 the Franken Berry cereal was released in America. The red colouring of the cereal could not be broken down by the body, and resulted in hundreds of children being hospitalised for passing stools that looked like strawberry ice cream, known as the Franken Berry Stool.

Astronauts ate Kellogg's Cornflakes aboard Apollo 11, the first moon landing.

Cap'n Crunch's full name is Horatio Magellan Crunch, and he was born on Crunch Island in the Sea of Milk.

In June 2006, a story went viral that the boy from the Frosties 'It's gonna taste great' TV commercial had committed suicide after being heavily bullied because of the advert. This was, in fact, false, and the boy is fine and well, and living in South Africa where he works as a professional gymnast.

Snap, Crackle and Pop have a brother named 'Pow'.

Toys were first introduced into cereal boxes in 1909 by Kellogg's, when 'The funny jungland of moving pictures' was given away with Cornflakes.

Special K is the best-selling UK cereal, followed by Weetabix.

21

FROSTY FLAKES MOJITO

Please join me in toasting my childhood teacher and best friend. He helped me learn how to swim and awarded me a badge with every length. He gave me a reflector for my bike when my stabilisers were removed. He was there to feed my post-school snack attacks. He was the greatest teacher: Tony the Tiger, we salute you!

Now Tony is going to help you get a wee bit drunk. What a guy! Another 90s icon you wish you could've been friends with was Mr Blobby. He was uncontrollable, he somehow managed to cause complete carnage wherever he went, and everyone seemed to love him – despite the fact he could only speak in Blobby language: blobby blobby blobby BLOBBY, and he was sooo annoying.

I wonder what he is doing now? I imagine he would make a good bouncer in a bar, and at closing time he would come out and scream 'BLOBBY BLOBBY BLOBBY', jumping on and trampling people and pushing them out of the bar, while everyone thinks, 'Awwww, Mr Blobby. He's so funny.' Come to think of it, you never actually see the banker on Deal or No Deal, so it's quite likely that Noel has re-hired his old work buddy as the faceless banker!

MAKES 1 DRINK

For the frosted flake and mint syrup

- 300g mint leaves, plus a few sprigs to decorate
- 200g Frosties, plus a few extra to decorate
- sugar, to taste (optional)

- 50ml white rum (Havana)
- 20ml lime juice
- Ice
- Soda water, to top up

Pour 400ml of water into a saucepan and add the mint leaves and the Frosties. Bring to the boil and let simmer for 10 minutes, then taste. If Tony isn't sweet enough for you, add more sugar, 50g at a time, but don't go crazy as you probably like having teeth. Once the time is up, remove the pan from the heat and pass the contents through a muslin cloth (if you don't have a muslin cloth, a fine sieve and sheet of Bounty is a poor man's alternative!). And there you go: syrup.

Pour 20ml of the syrup, the rum and lime juice, over ice in a cocktail shaker and shake it like Tom Cruise in that film that he shook up drinks in. What do you call it? Oh yeah, Bridget Jones.

Now pour into a long glass and garnish with a few mint sprigs and a few flakes of Frosties, and raise a toast to Tony.

GRANOLA TOM COLLINS

Tom, Jack, Jerry, Jim, Gordon, José and Johnnie. I've spent many a night with these men, and sometimes I've really taken a pounding, going back and forth between them. At the end of it, I have to be honest, I've usually found it hard to walk. Which is why you shouldn't mix your drinks...

MAKES 1 DRINK

For the granola syrup
- 500g gooseberries (fresh or frozen)
- 150g of your favourite granola
- 340ml Hoegaarden

- Ice, to serve
- 50ml Old Tom gin (add a teaspoon of sugar to every 100ml of London Dry Gin if you can't find Old Tom)
- 20ml lemon juice
- Hoegaarden or other wheat beer, to top up
- Physalis, to decorate

First you need to make your granola syrup. Put the gooseberries (if using frozen, make sure they are thawed) into a pan with the granola and Hoegaarden and simmer for 5 minutes, stirring regularly, then bring to the boil for 1 minute, take off the heat and let cool. Once cool, strain the mixture and – hey presto – there's your granola syrup.

Now take 20ml of the syrup and pour over ice with the gin and lemon juice into a tall glass, and top up with the Hoegaarden. Decorate with a physalis (it's a super fancy fruit that'll take your cocktail from home-made to cocktail bar in a flash!), some granola and a straw. You're ready to rock 'n' roll!

A Fruit Loops Playlist

1. 'Saved By The Bell Theme'
   Silver Screen Symphony
2. 'You Make My Dreams'
   Hall & Oates
3. 'Johnny B Good'
   Chuck Berry
4. 'How Bizarre'
   OMC

WHAT YOUR FAVOURITE CEREAL SAYS ABOUT YOU

KRAVE you are very good at keeping secrets, but you can also hide your problems. But be careful not to bottle too much up as when you let the truth out, it can be pretty intense.

WEETABIX you like to play it safe, when you play Mario Kart you are always Mario and never Wario. If you were a cheese, you'd be Cheddar. You sit on the fence so much, people think you are a caterpillar.

CORNFLAKES you don't like anyone having fun around you, you are a fun sponge, at parties you suck the fun out like a personality Hoover.

COCO POPS you were very popular in school, but things have gone downhill since; you've found it hard to get used to the fact that you peaked in high school. People still like you but in smaller doses.

COOKIE CRISP you're a daredevil, you'll be the one to suggest skinny dipping, but then let others do it first and steal their clothes. In truth or dare you always choose double dare.

RICICLES you use your childishness to get out of sticky situations, and often speak in a baby voice. When on the toilet you dry wipe twice, then wet wipe once.

GRANOLA you lost your virginity when you were 15 but told people it was when you were 22. You play netball at the weekends and think it gives you an edge.

CURIOUSLY CINNAMON you kissed a girl in college and insist you are bisexual, although you would never actually have a relationship with another woman; you are totally barsexual.

SUGAR PUFFS HONEY MONSTER PUFFS you are trying to be someone you are not, despite many attempts to make yourself seem 'normal' you'll still be an emo and should embrace it.

CRUNCHY NUT CORNFLAKES you're the kooky person at work, people know you'll have a wacky theme for the Xmas party like dead celebrity nuns in drag. Btw people love your vintage lunchbox.

LUCKY CHARMS you tell people you are Irish every St Patrick's Day but the most Irish you've had in you is Paddy O'Doherty when you went to that hen night in Dublin in 2004.

CHEERIOS you're so frigid, very clean living, but give you a drink and you let your hair down, pissing on lamp posts and shouting at the drive-thru in McDonald's, when it's closed.

SHREDDED WHEAT you consider yourself well travelled, but a weekend in Benidorm once a year contradicts this.

DON'T LIKE CEREAL? you are dead inside, have gonorrhea, and cannot be trusted.

TOP 5 TOYS

1. **Boglins**
2. **Dream Phone**
3. **Teddy Ruxpin**
4. **Gak**
5. **My Pet Monster**

TOP 5 MEALS

1. **Breakfast – 28th September 2002**
2. **Dinner – 23rd January 2006**
3. **Dinner – 6th May 2006**
4. **Lunch – 19th February 1999**
5. **Dinner – 11th October 2012**

ESPRESSO PEANUTTINI

Sometimes getting drunk is exhausting. Do you ever feel like you need a wee energy boost to get you through the next few drinks? And yes, a jägerbomb could do the trick, but you're not chugging down shots like you're on a binge-drinking Magaluf weekend; you want to remain classy. So the espresso martini will keep you awake, drunk and, best of all, swanky as f**k.

Of course, it wouldn't be Cereal Killer without adding some cereal in there somewhere. If you haven't heard of Reese's Puffs before, by god you are in for a treat. It's a peanut butter cereal, mmm, peanut butter. Those crazy Americans again! You'll be able to pick this cereal up online or in specialist American candy stores, and you'll never want to eat a non-peanut-butter cereal again!

It's quite an easy cocktail to make, meaning the classiness levels are high with effort levels remaining low. It's win-win.

MAKES 1 DRINK
For the Amaretto infusion
- Couple of handfuls of Reese's Puffs, plus a few to decorate
- 20ml Amaretto

- 30ml vanilla vodka (Absolut, but Stoli will do)
- 20ml Kahlúa
- 25ml fresh espresso
- Ice, to serve

Stick the Reese's Puffs in a bowl with the Amaretto — the Amaretto is going to get involved with the <u>mind-blowing peanut flavour</u> of the Reese's — and set aside to infuse (room temperature is perfect for this).

After an hour, strain the liquid through a sieve set over a jug. You can leave it to infuse for longer if you wish, but make sure it doesn't get all mushy. If it does, use some muslin or cheesecloth.

Pour 20ml of the infusion into a cocktail shaker with all the other ingredients and a few ice cubes, and start shaking (flare bartending is not advised, unless it's your sixth cocktail, at which point flare bartending is highly recommended). Now strain into a martini glass and decorate with three Reese's Puffs perched in the <u>foamy head</u>, on a cocktail stick.

HONEY PUFF CHAMOMILE TEA

The name really isn't sticking, but it did take a while to get used to calling a Marathon a 'Snickers', Opal Fruits 'Starburst' and Michael Jackson white, so let's stick with it.

I'm sure if the Honey Monster ever hit the bottle (which I'm sure he doesn't. I see the Honey Monster as an ex-alcoholic – just look at him in the '70s, he was definitely on something, but I'm glad he came out the other side) he'd be a gin drinker. Some people say 'gin makes you sin', and that's bullshit, gin makes you drunk and drunk makes you sin. But I guess 'gin makes you drunk' doesn't have the same ring to it.

MAKES 1 DRINK

For the gin/Honey Monster Puff/tea infusion

- 200ml gin
- 2 chamomile teabags
- 1 tablespoon fruity jam (any would do, but raspberry or passionfruit would be awesome)
- 6 tablespoons Honey Monster Puffs
- 1 lemon

- 40ml Noilly Prat
- 20ml lemon juice
- 2 dashes grapefruit bitters (would be great here if you have some)
- 10ml sugar syrup (just one to one, 5ml each of sugar and water)
- ice, to serve
- grapefruit wedge, to serve

Pop the gin into a bowl with the chamomile teabags, the fruity jam and the Honey Monster Puffs. Leave all these ingredients to really get involved with each other for 20 minutes, then scoop out the cereal. Add one massive piece of peel from the lemon to the jam, tea and gin mixture and leave to infuse for another 20 minutes.

Strain the liquid after 20 minutes and add 25ml of it to the Noilly Prat, lemon juice, grapefruit bitters (if using) and sugar syrup. It's important to say do not use Martini Extra Dry here, for reasons only Billy knows! Now shake it all up in a cocktail shaker and serve over ice in a wine glass, with a grapefruit wedge and some Honey Monster Puffs pinned to the side of the glass using the juice from the grapefruit wedge.

A Fruit Loops Playlist

5. 'All That She Wants'
   Ace of Base

6. 'Connection'
   Elastica

7. 'Trash'
   Suede

8. 'Girls and Boys'
   Blur

THE PERFECT BOWL OF CEREAL

TEMPERATURES

MILK
3° and straight out of the fridge. For best results use whole milk.

ROOM
Should be 20°, this will mean there will be no outside temperature distractions, meaning the experience of the cold milk hitting body temperature will be at optimum pleasure.

BOWL SHAPE
Semi-spherical bowl shape is the ultimate for spoon scoopage.

SPOON SHAPE
Cream soup spoon, ultimate partner for semi-spherical bowl, spoon glides seamlessly along base of bowl.

FRESHLY OPENED CEREAL
Cereal loses flavour after opening the air-sealed bag. Cereal is at optimum flavour and crunch for 1.5 hours after opening.

KILLER CEREAL

CEREAL AMOUNT

Depending on size and appetite, cereal should always be consumed as 1.2 parts milk, 2 parts cereal based on cubic volume not weight.

CLOTHING

Clothing should be loose-fitting jersey material.

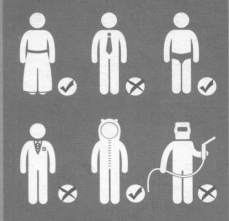

TIME

Best time for eating cereal is between 8:00 - 8:25am and 10:40 - 11:15pm.

fig.1   fig.2

ANGLE

Milk should be poured into cereal, never the other way around, and should be poured in at a height of 9cm from the top of the cereal, into the area called the milk ring, which is 25% in from the side, and 25% out from the centre of the bowl.

fig.1

9cm

fig.2

MILK RING

CEREAL COCKTAILS

BANANARAMA

#1 Get some bananas
#2 Choose a banana
#3 Peal the banana
#4 Eat the banana

The only rule I stick to when eating bananas is to never eat one in public. And if this is unavoidable, making eye contact while eating the banana is an absolute no no.

Banana and Nutella marry together perfectly, like Scott and Charlene (these 2 Aussies, although no longer in Neighbours, now have 2 kids, and live in Brisbane, the perfect happily-ever-after TV couple).

As I recall, everything in my teenage years had a layer of Nutella on it, I was absolutely obsessed with the stuff. Nutella on toast was number 1, followed by Nutella stirred into a cup of tea, and then Nutella 'neat' (eaten from the jar with a spoon) and Nutella 'soup' (heated in the microwave then eaten with a spoon).

Party fact: Nutella uses 25 per cent of the world's supply of hazelnuts. I think during my youth I probably consumed 10 per cent of the world's hazelnuts. Pouring our cereal cocktails is a lot like drowning – they are so easy, even a child could do it.

2 SERVINGS

- 1 bowl of Weetabix Crispy Minis Banana approx. 40g
- ½ ripe banana, chopped down the middle then sliced into bite-sized half circles
- 2 tablespoons Nutella
- 150ml whole milk
- 1 tablespoon Crusha Banana milkshake syrup
- 1 foam banana, to decorate

Fill your bowl three-quarters full with the cereal and scatter the chopped banana on top. Spoon the Nutella into a piping bag and pipe a swirl starting from the outside of the bowl; this looks best, but if you're not trying to impress anyone then a few spoonfuls dotted over the top works fine.

Mix up your banana milk – not too strong as you've a lot of banana going on already – and drench your cereal. Finally, pop a foam banana on top of the cereal to decorate and you're good to go!

If you like coffee with your cereal, then why not hit two birds with one spoon and have coffee in your cereal? We heard that in Spain it's common to pour coffee over your cereal (source: the internet, not sure which page, but the internet never lies). This inspired us to do something similar.

When Friends first hit our screens in the 90s, there was nothing cooler than going to a coffee shop and sitting on a sofa – and I mean people used to queue for sofas. Everyone would also play the 'which Friends character are you?' game and this was way before BuzzFeed could do the work for you. We all had that friend that thought they were a Phoebe, but were in fact a total Monica, and got really angry at the fact everyone thought they were a Monica, which is such a Monica thing to do.

2 SERVINGS

- ½ bowl of Nesquik cereal approx. 20g
- ½ bowl of Coco Pops approx. 20g
- ½ Flake, crushed
- Instant coffee granules mixed with 1 teaspoon of boiling water
- 150ml whole milk
- 1 café straw, to serve

This cocktail is about as middle class as a cereal can get – it's got a bloody café straw in it! So get your bowl ready and fill it three-quarters full with the Nesquik cereal first, then add the Coco Pops and swirl the cereal in a circular motion – this will allow the Nesquik to peek through the sea of Coco Pops.

Scatter the crushed Flake over the top and pop in your café straw. It looks right posh now, doesn't it?

Add 1 teaspoon of the blended coffee to your milk and mix well. Now pour this over the cereal and enjoy.

The sofa from Friends!

BOWLOCINNO

CHOCOPOTOMUS

A **Fruit Loops Playlist**

9. 'Peaches'
   The Presidents of the
   United States of America

10. 'Together In Electric Dreams'
    The Human League

11. 'All She Wants To
    Do Is Dance'
    Don Henley

12. 'Walk Like A Panther'
    Cool Sensation

The Chocopotomus is the café's signature dish — surprisingly we haven't won a Michelin star yet. Not sure why, but when we do, it'll probably be for this.

This little hippo has celebrity fans, too — Amanda Holden gorged down the hippo's chocolatey backside live on This Morning, and we heard a rumour that the Queen chomps down on this combination every Saturday morning while watching SpongeBob SquarePants in her onesie. That's from a very reliable source, btw.

This bowl will bring out the biggest kid in all of us. I served this to my dad and within minutes he was jumping on the sofa, wiping faeces on the walls and hammering his Lego into my iPad screen.

MAKES 1 BOWL

- ½ bowl of Krave Milk Chocolate approx. 20g
- ½ bowl of Coco Pops approx. 20g
- 1 Happy Hippo
- 150ml whole milk
- 1 tablespoon of Crusha Chocolate Milkshake Mix/ Hershey's Chocolate Syrup

The weights suggested are just guidelines — it all depends on the size of the mouth being fed. You could make a swamp with an entire family of hippos in a massive mixing bowl if you're feeling more than peckish, or have just downloaded the entire first season of Saved by the Bell (highly recommended).

So, get your bowl of choice and add the Krave first, then the Coco Pops and swirl the bowl to reveal those little pillows of happiness.

Pop in the hippo and jiggle him down — you want this wee man to be wallowing in his swamp.

Get your milk shaken up with the chocolate flavouring to the level of chocolateyness you desire, then pour it into the hippo's swamp, and enjoy.

MAGIC EYES

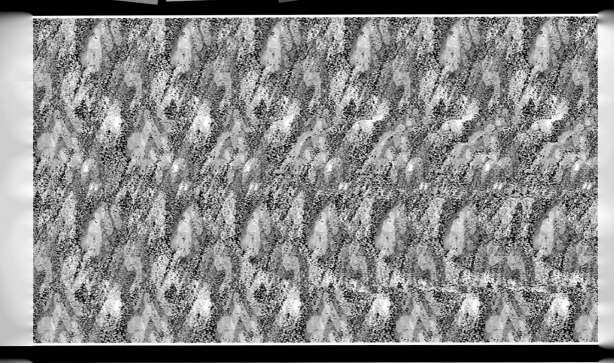

If you stare at each of these images, one at a time, until your eyes go woozy, the image will then go all **3-D** on you. You should then see a hidden image or message in each one!

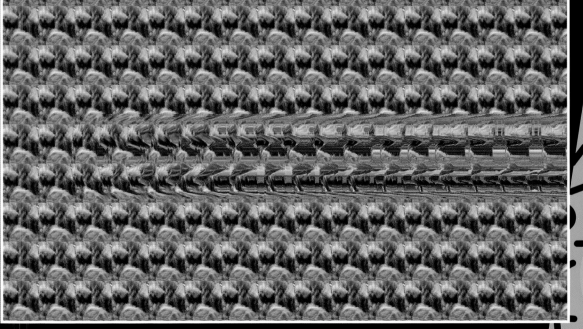

If you have any sort of nut allergy you should probably look away now. Just reading this recipe may induce a reaction.

The Feckin' Nutcase (best said in an Irish accent) is for people who love putting nuts in their mouths. I, for one, am a fan of this, and the multiple textures this combo gives you is like a crunchy surprise for the palate.

This cocktail tastes best made with almond milk, which often raises the question, how do you milk an almond? TBH, I don't know or particularly care, but I do know that it tastes great. And you may be surprised at the sheer amount of 'milks' now available: rice, oat, coconut, hazelnut, soya ... the list goes on, but what will we be milking next? Armchairs? Mobile phones? Goats? What a world, eh?!

MAKES 1 BOWL
- ⅓ bowl Honey Cheerios approx. 15g
- ⅓ bowl Crunchy Nut Cornflakes approx. 15g
- ⅓ bowl Crunchy Nut Clusters approx. 15g
- 10 hazelnuts, roughly chopped
- 150ml almond milk

Choose your nutty receptacle and layer on the three cereals starting with the Cheerios, then the Crunchy Nut Cornflakes, and finally the Clusters. We find the Clusters work better when broken down from the cluster form into smaller bits. Give the cereals a clockwise swirl to mix them up.

Scatter over the hazelnuts generously, then pour over the almond milk and sit back and enjoy a gob full of feckin' nuts.

FECKIN' NUTCASE

KING
OF THE LIONS

Naaaants een-vwen-yaaaaaa ma-ba-gee-chi-ba-va

If this makes any sense to you, you'll probably be singing this song for the rest of the day. And a kick-ass soundtrack like The Lion King should definitely be enjoyed while eating this cereal cocktail.

The Lion King movie brought us many things as children: 'hakuna matata' was used on a daily basis, whether it made sense or not. 'Boys, have you done your homework?', 'hakuna matata'. The death of Mufasa; I'm not sure why Disney thought it acceptable to put us through this trauma at such a young age, but it made me realise Scar was a royal dick, and not everyone in life will be a Disney f***ing prince! And lastly, Timon and Pumbaa, one of the best onscreen representations of gay parenting.

MAKES 1 BOWL
- ½ bowl of Coco Caramel Shreddies cereal about 20g
- ½ bowl of Lion Bar cereal about 20g
- 7 Mars mix balls
- 1 tablespoon caramel syrup (used as ice-cream topping)
- 150ml whole milk

First off, put the Coco Caramel Shreddies into your desired bowl, then top up with the Lion Bar cereal. Swirl the cereals in a circular motion; this will reveal the Shreddies through the Lion, a must when mixing two cereals.

Now, throw on a handful of Mars mix balls, shake your milk up with the caramel syrup, pour over and enjoy. And if you get any of the measurements wrong, hakuna matata, it'll still taste great anyway.

We have seen all kinds of people come into our café: Jesus came in December for a pre-birthday snack; we've had people queue for an hour just to order toast; it has been known for people to order 4 bowls in one sitting; and people who don't like milk is quite a common occurrence. Some like to eat cereal dry, others like to have cereal with water, we have even had requests to butter a Weetabix for a customer. But one milk alternative that is surprisingly delicious is orange juice.

This combo can turn some people's stomachs, but don't be so quick to dismiss it. The Coco Shreddies with the OJ has a chocolate-orange taste, but without the creaminess of a chocolate bar. The Jaffa Cakes complement the contrast perfectly and when the juice hits the sponge and it soaks it up, it becomes a sloppy mess of tastiness.

2 SERVINGS
- 1 x bowl of Coco Shreddies
- 2 x Jaffa Cakes
- 150ml orange juice

This interesting mix couldn't be easier, in fact I think it might be quite patronising explaining the recipe. So I'll make it rhyme....

Get your bowl, and in goes the cereal.
Add the Jaffa Cakes, it really is that simple.
Pour over the OJ, and try not to be cynical.
Get yourself a spoon, I hope you liked my lyricals.

Fruit Loops Playlist

13. 'God Gave Rock 'n' Roll To You II'
    KISS

14. 'Cherry Bomb'
    The Runaways

15. 'Oh Yeah'
    Yello

16. 'The Wild Boys'
    Duran Duran

ORANGE YOU GLAD
I DIDN'T ORDER MILK

S'MORE THAN WORDS

Americans have some pretty American foods: chilli dogs, pumpkin pie, pb&j, Twinkies, meatloaf (not the singer) and cheese in a can. But there are few things more American than sitting around a campfire toasting marshmallows for your s'mores (party fact: they are named s'mores due to the frequent requests for 'some more' once made). Now all you need is a gun, a big gulp, a Bruce Springsteen CD, no NHS, and you are living the 'murican dream!

The Golden Grahams in this cocktail are a particular childhood favourite of mine. The 90s were strewn with sugar treats like Wham bars, Dip Dabs and Opal Fruits (now Starburst), so when the 90s finished and Golden Grahams were banned for their high sugar content, my heart broke into honey and brown sugar ridged squares. But I can only thank the cereal gods for hearing the cries of the nation, because this delicious cereal was remade in 2010 – this time with wholegrain and less sugar. But we'll accept that.

MAKES 1 BOWL
- 1 bowl of Golden Grahams approx. 40g
- 20 small white marshmallows
- 150ml whole milk
- Crusha Chocolate Flavour Milkshake mix
- Campfire (optional)

Fill your bowl with those delicious shiny squares of Grahams, and then scatter the marshmallows over the top – there's no need for toasting, unless you are feeling adventurous.

Mix up the chocolate milk to your preference, following the instructions on the packaging, pour it over the cereal, sit down on a log and start singing 'Bye bye, Miss American Pie'.

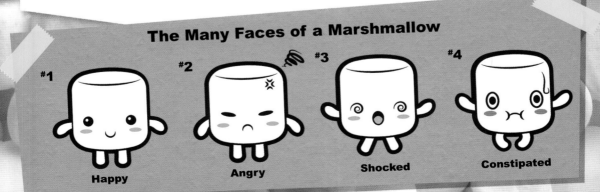

The Many Faces of a Marshmallow

#1 Happy
#2 Angry
#3 Shocked
#4 Constipated

Ordinarily when you mention poop, it's not something that induces lip licking, but when you talk about the mythical unicorn's bowel movements, it can fill us with joy and wonder. And if you just have a look at this sensational cocktail, you'll see exactly why the name is so apt. This is one meal that was made for Instagraming. Pop on an 'x-pro II', adjust the vignette and tilt-shift the absolute s**t out of it, and watch the 'likes' come rolling in*.

I now know unicorns do not exist, but when I was in primary school there was this guy named Jonathon who had me convinced not only that unicorns were real, but he had seen one with his own eyes, in his granny's back yard (I know, I was gullible). In hindsight, you should never trust someone that can't blow their own nose at the age of 9.

1 SERVING
- 1 bowl of Ricicles approx. 40g
- 3 broken party rings
- 15 mini marshmallows
- 1 tablespoon marshmallow fluff
- Sprinkling of hundreds and thousands
- 150ml semi-skimmed milk

Fill your bowl with Ricicles and give it a shake to flatten the surface of the cereal – a flat workspace is crucial to the positioning of the toppings and therefore total Instagram 'likes'. Now, place the broken party rings around the edge of the bowl, ensuring they are icing side up, and scatter the marshmallows around the same area, leaving a topping-free space in the middle of the bowl.

Now, you can either put the fluff into a piping bag and pipe the most perfect little poop into the centre of the bowl, but let's be honest, this is extra washing up, and it's all going to come out the same colour anyway, so you could just scoop it in straight from the jar with a spoon.

Sprinkle the newly formed poop with hundreds and thousands and pour over the milk. This cocktail is as sweet as a puppy and a kitten kissing, but if you want to up the sweetness, make it with strawberry milk.

*'likes' not guaranteed

ANYONE FOR A PARTY?

UNICORN POOP

EVOLUTION OF THE HONEY MONSTER

No one really knows exactly where he came from, but Honey Monster (HM) has been around since 1976 and the big guy has always had a kind of yellow, hairy look going on, although he did go through a brief, ill-advised Gordon the Gopher phase in one of his incarnations (see above). Thankfully, he was soon back to good old yellow.

Eat enough Sugar Puffs and you'll end up looking like me.

You too can be covered in super badges and grow big and handsome like me. Because in every special pack of Sugar Puffs, there's a free stick-on Honey Monster badge.

As well as lots of my favourite breakfast. And as there are four badges to collect, get your mummy to buy lots of Sugar Puffs in the special packs.

Oh, I bet you thought that I'd forgotten to tell you about the honey? Well, I just have! He! He!

Tell 'em about the honey... Yummy!

Everyone loved HM and it was the joyful anarchy he brought to cereals that we loved most. When he rumbled, 'Tell 'em about the honey, Mummy' on TV to actor Henry McGee and McGee then said, 'I'm not his Mummy,' HM trashed the set. Seems fair.

Tell 'em about the honey, mummy!

Some TV ads actually showed kids deprived of their Sugar Puffs (as they were then) turning into Honey Monsters, and that may explain where he came from. But even if he started out as a normal, humble child, he was soon rubbing shoulders (and he's got plenty to rub) with the rich and famous. Rumour has it that HM turned down the role of Chewbacca in *Star Wars* because his shoulders wouldn't fit in the Millennium Falcon.

In 1996, Newcastle United manager Kevin Keegan signed up HM – a shrewd move on Keegan's part as, within a couple of years, he was manager of England. HM's reward for his years of faithful service came in 2014, when his breakfast cereal was renamed in his honour – Sugar Puffs became Honey Monster Puffs. Those who found the new name difficult to swallow soon got used to it. After all, gentle and lovable as he is, who's going to argue with a seven-foot-tall yellow hairy monster?

SAVOURY STUFF

Pop tarts were the perfect accompaniment to our bowl of cereal when we were kids. There was something very bodacious about the speckled frosting on the toaster pastries that made us feel like American teenagers, just like 'Clarissa' in her 'explains it all' series. Which, in hindsight, didn't really explain it all to us; we did learn about dealing with pimples and wearing a training bra (not that I needed that knowledge), but there was a plethora of subjects that Clarissa left unexplained – global politics, art history, quantum physics...

One thing Clarissa did explain, though, has stuck with me: there is nothing cooler than having a bedroom window that your best friend could climb through to come and see you. But in the real world, how goddamn dangerous is that?!

Back to pop tarts, and I'm sure you are already salivating at the thought of a bacon one... Mixing savoury bacon with something sweet isn't a new thing; in America, Dunkin' Donuts even sell a breakfast donut, which is essentially a bacon butty made from a glazed donut instead of a bread roll. Too far?

MAKES 4

- 8 rashers streaky bacon (keep 1 rasher separate for the garnish)
- 100ml maple syrup (plus a few teaspoons extra for the maple glaze)
- 320g store-bought shortcrust pastry
- 1 egg, beaten
- 100g icing sugar

OK, first up, preheat the oven to 180°C and heat the grill. Everything else in this recipe will be much more pleasurable if you are working to the smell of grilled bacon.

Grill the bacon until crispy and brown, and pop 7 of the 8 rashers into your food processor, along with the maple syrup (keeping 1 for garnishing the tarts) and pulse it, pulse it good, p-pulse it real good, until smooth.

If you're a Miss Fancy Pants and have a pasta roller, this is the time to use it; if you're a regular Joe, a rolling pin or empty wine bottle will suffice. Now roll out the pastry to the thickness of a penny, and cut it into 8 pop-tart-sized rectangles (4 for the base and 4 for the lids).

Lay out the pastry rectangles on a baking tray lined with baking parchment and brush the edges of the pastry with the beaten egg. Top half of the rectangles with the tasty bacon paste, leaving a 1cm gap right around the edges, then pop another pastry rectangle on top and seal the edges by pressing down with a fork.

Bake in the oven for 15 minutes, or until golden brown. Take them out of the oven and try to resist scoffing them, instead let them cool.

While the tarts are cooling, sift the icing sugar into a bowl then slowly add some maple syrup, one teaspoon at a time, stirring until it is smooth like Luther Vandross. Now spread the maple icing on top of the tarts, and finely chop the extra grilled bacon and sprinkle on top.

All that's left to do is take the pop tarts to a friend's house and try to climb through the window without getting arrested!

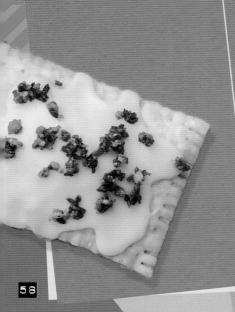

BACON POP TART

1
1
4
5
2
3
1
2
6
3
2
1
1
2
4
1
5
1
1
1
3

Find Your Way to the
CEREAL KILLER CAFÉ

Fancy a bowl of cereal? All you have to do is pop down to the Cereal Killer Café. The usual thing to do in a game like this is to start at the beginning and take turns to throw dice to see how many squares you can go forward – but who can ever find dice when you need them? Instead, with the book flattened out as best you can, hold a spoon handle-side down, circle the 'game board' round and round several times with your eyes shut and stab the handle at the edge to choose a number.

You can then move your counter – for counters you can use a Sugar Puff, a Bitesize Shreddie, a Frostie (too bad if someone else lands on your square and smashes you into crumbs), a 5p piece, a toenail clipping – anything that will fit on the squares.

Then you just follow the instructions on the squares you land on – or not, if there aren't any – and the first one to reach us in the café is the winner!

START!

An Umbongo truck crashes and you surf **forward two squares** on a tropical juice tsunami.

You decide to go by bike. **Move on two squares** for being green.

Slip on spilt milk and bruise your coccyx. **Miss a turn** with your bum in a sling.

Your bike is a Raleigh Chopper – cool but **VERY** slow. **Miss a turn.**

CHEERY GRILLED CHEESE SANDWICH

Grilled cheese sandwiches are pretty amazing – who'd have thought some bread, cheese and a sliver of butter could make you salivate more than Homer Simpson over a box of doughnuts? Well, I'm going to tell you that you can take your grilled cheese to the next level. Adding Cheerios into the mix gives a new layer of amazingness. CRUNCH! Yep, those Cheerios become BFFs with the bread and the result is something else. This is such an easy recipe – mostly made after a few pints of the black stuff, and any drunk food needs to be quick, easy and bloody tasty.

2 SERVINGS

- 1 block of cheese (you'll probably not need the whole block, unless you really like cheese)
- 4 slices of bread (whatever your preference – we prefer a classic white medium cut)
- Sliced ham (we like the fancy ham you get with the breadcrumbs round the edge)
- A wee bit of butter, for spreading
- 2 fistfuls of Cheerios

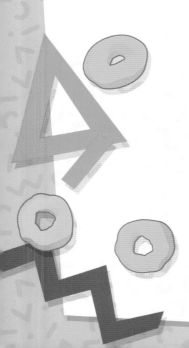

You'll need to slice some cheese and grate a bit as well – enough slices to cover two slices of bread, and the same amount grated. Put the cheese to one side.

Now get your greaseproof paper and rip out enough to fit around both sides of the bread, a bit like a book, with the bread being the pages. You don't want any overhang of the paper – I'll explain why later.

Get your new bread book and open up the centre pages, then place your sliced cheese on one slice of the bread, along with your ham (for a vegetarian option, lose the ham; for a vegan option, have an apple). Now close the book and butter the outside of your bread.

It's Cheerio time! Grab a handful of Cheerios and place them on the buttered side of the bread (it's good to get a bit OCD and evenly spread out the Cheerios for the perfect crunch every time) and sprinkle over a quarter of the grated cheese, then cover with the greaseproof paper, flip, and repeat. Press down on the front cover to make sure all the layers are connected.

Now your book should read like this: greaseproof paper, cheese, Cheerios, butter, bread, ham, cheese, bread, butter, Cheerios, cheese, greaseproof paper. A classic! Now you're ready to heat up this foodgasm. Get a hot frying pan ready on a high heat and place your sandwich in the centre of the pan (this is why it's important not to have overhang on your greaseproof paper – fire + paper = 1 smoke-filled flat and some very angry flatmates. We can speak from experience here). Now gently press your sandwich with a spatula, then flip and press, flip and press, for approximately 5 minutes or until the outside of the sandwich is golden brown. This is when the mouth is at maximum saliva capacity.

Now you are ready to serve, so choose whether to cut the sandwiches into squares, rectangles or triangles. We always have 4 triangles because 4 small triangles seem like more than 2 larger ones, and the more food you have the better, right?

THE PARTY HEDGEHOG

No party in the 90s was complete without a cheese hedgehog, so this just had to go into the book. Normally I would never consider eating cheese with a wedge of pineapple (although it's not as bad as pineapple on a pizza – that should be illegal), but this recipe somehow makes sense. And when that hedgehog is staring up at you, with his big doughy eyes, begging you to nibble on his fruitful spines, how can you resist?

Kids' birthday parties in the 90s were without shame. There were three places every kid wanted to hold their party, and usually in this order:

1. Soft play area, rubbish name for what it is: ball pits, slides and swings. Holy moly! It was heaven, although when I think of one now, all I can think of is the smell of kids' feet – gross out!
2. Laser quest – black lights in a dark room with neon paint. So rad!
3. McDonald's or Burger King (if you got invited to a Wimpy party, you knew the kid's parents really hated them)

I remember one kid at our school had a party which involved all of the top three. Last I heard he was in jail for making fraudulent passports, and that is proof as to why you can have too much of a good thing.

1 HEDGEHOG CAN SERVE UP TO 8 PEOPLE DEPENDING ON WHAT ELSE IS ON OFFER AT THE PARTY!

- 1 orange, halved
- 1 block of cheese, cubed
- 1 large handful Cheerios
- 1 can pineapple rings, cubed
- 1 jar pickled onions, halved
- 1 olive, halved
- 1 mushroom
- Cocktail sticks, to decorate

Get one of your orange halves and cover it in tin foil, moulding the front into a point for Mr Hedgehog's face. Now with each spike you should alternate the following:

1. Cheese-Cheerio-pineapple cube
2. Cheese-Cheerio-onion

Repeat, to cover the entire back of your hedgehog. Now some artistic flair can come in handy here: use two olive halves for the eyes, then slice a mushroom, using the stem for the nose and the cup for the mouth.

Possible names for your new friend:
- Pokey McSpikerston
- Professor Prickles
- Spike Lee
- Dr Cuddlebottoms
- Dave

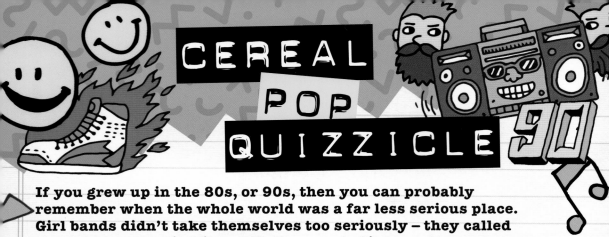

CEREAL POP QUIZZICLE

If you grew up in the 80s, or 90s, then you can probably remember when the whole world was a far less serious place. Girl bands didn't take themselves too seriously – they called themselves Atomic Kitten, Shakespear's Sister or Bananarama, and boy bands weren't that much more sensible, calling themselves Adam and the Ants, 5ive or Kajagoogoo.

Those were the days, but how much can you remember about those poptastic times and, more to the point in a book written around cereal, what's your knowledge of crispy, crunchy, wheaty and flaky things like?

Try this Pop Cereal Quizzicle to find out!

1. **The twins from Fun House were called**
   a) Gary and Alan
   b) Melanie and Martina
   c) Mel and Sue

2. **Complete the song title 'Reach for the...'**
   a) Cornflakes
   b) Stars
   c) Perfect body weight you haven't had since your early 20s

3. **Victoria Adams is better known as who?**
   a) Posh Spice
   b) Roland Rat
   c) Victoria Wood

4. **What were the zones in the Crystal Maze?**
   a) Aztec, Industrial, Futuristic, Medieval
   b) Earth, wind, fire, water
   c) North, south, east, west

5. **Weetabix tastes better with**
   a) Sugar
   b) Sugar
   c) Sugar

6. **Bill and Ted's surnames were**
   a) Righteous and Excellent
   b) Esquire and Theodore
   c) Preston and Logan

7. **The members of Wham! are**
   a) George Michael and the other one
   b) Andrew Ridgeley and George Michael
   c) George Michael and George Michael

8. **In what year did Scott and Charlene get married in Neighbours?**
a) 1988
b) 1991
c) 1983

9. **How many different types of Cheerio are there in one bowl?**
a) 1 and they're all round
b) 3: brown, a lighter brown and an even lighter one
c) 4 delicious wholegrains

10. **Gordon the Gopher's sidekick was**
a) Pat Sharp
b) Phillip Schofield
c) Andy Peters

11. **Where was Baywatch set?**
a) Malibu
b) Miami
c) California

12. **East 17 had a hit with**
a) 'Relight My Doob'
b) 'It's Alright'
c) 'Stop'

13. **What number am I thinking of?**
a) 1
b) 86
c) 23

14. **PJ and Duncan hailed from which TV show?**
a) Home and Away
b) Byker Grove
c) Grange Hill

15. **Complete this famous All Saints lyric – 'Never ever have I ever felt so...'**
a) Cold
b) Sad
c) Fat

16. **What colour is Tony the Tiger's nose?**
a) Red
b) Black
c) Blue

17. **Badger from Bodger and Badger likes what?**
a) Lasagne
b) Paninis
c) Mashed potato

18. **Mr Blobby's Christmas number one was called**
a) 'The Blobby Song'
b) 'Blobby Blobby Blobby'
c) 'Mr Blobby'

19. **How do you summon an unwanted dead person?**
a) Beetlejuice
b) Beetlejuice
c) Beetlejuice

20. **What were the two twins from Sister Sister called?**
a) Tina and Tanya
b) Gary and Alan
c) Tia and Tamera

PARTY

Cornflakes or, as I call them, naked Frosties, aren't the tastiest of cereals, in fact they're pretty basic, so it's hard to get excited about them. Until now, of course.

Cornflake chicken is next-level good, so good, in fact, that it deserves its own song:

> Golden crispy crunchy chicken
> You're a bug that has me bitten
> You look so rad in your cornflake jacket
> I want to eat you, while also wearing a jacket.

Scrap the song, let's just make some chicken...

4 SERVINGS
- Plain flour, seasoned with salt and black pepper, for dusting
- 2 eggs, beaten
- 125g cornflakes, crushed or blended to the consistency of rock salt
- 1 tablespoon cayenne pepper
- 1 teaspoon garlic powder
- 500g chicken breast, sliced into strips

First, get out three bowls for the dipping of the chicken. In bowl 1 add the seasoned flour; in bowl 2, the eggs; and in bowl 3, the crushed cornflakes mixed with the cayenne and garlic.

Now have a greased baking tray ready and preheat the oven to 200°C. Get your bowls in a row and get your chicken ready to dip dip dip – it's like a chicken assault course! First, roll that chicken into the flour, rolling until every inch of it is covered. Next, dip it into the egg, and again roll it round and cover the whole piece of chicken. Finally, roll it into the cornflake mix. Your fingers should be pretty sticky by now, but I have to tell you, it's going to get worse before it gets better!

Place the cornflaked chicken onto the baking tray and repeat the dipping until all your chicken bits are lined up and ready to hit the oven. Bake the chicken for 30 minutes until golden brown and the chicken is cooked through.

Serve with your choice of condiment. I'd recommend: ketchup, mayo, hot sauce, hot sauce mixed with ketchup, brown sauce, Reggae Reggae sauce, garlic and herb – actually I'd recommend all of the condiments, all of them, except tartar sauce. There is not now, and there will never be, a time that you should eat tartar sauce.

CORNFLAKE CHICKEN

CRUNCHY NUTTY ROAST

Nut roasts are usually reserved for vegans and hippies, but if you don't like a slab of meat on your plate, or feel your slab of meat could do with a side of something cereal-based, then 'kablamo'! Wrap your lips round this crunchy nut roast.

All the nuts in this recipe have been replaced with the best member of the Crunchy Nut family and, wowzer, lather this bad boy in gravy, serve with a side of roast potato and a few veg and you're only a couple of crackers and a turkey away from an Xmas dinner. Only this meal will not have to include bad cracker prizes (I once got a nipple ring in a cracker), any sort of druncle (drunk uncle) or another Royle Family Christmas special!!

4 SERVINGS

- Knob of butter
- 1 tablespoon olive oil
- ½ onion, finely chopped
- 1 celery stick, finely chopped
- 1 clove garlic, finely chopped
- ½ red pepper, deseeded and finely chopped
- ½ carrot, grated
- 100g red lentils
- 1 teaspoon smoked hot paprika
- 1 teaspoon dried mixed herbs
- 150ml vegetable stock
- 2 small eggs, beaten
- 100g cheddar cheese, grated
- 200g Crunchy Nut Clusters

OK, melt the butter in a frying pan on a low heat and add the oil, then the chopped onion, celery and garlic (life hack – stop your eyes from watering while cutting onions … by getting someone else to do it), and cook on a medium heat for 10 minutes until softened.

Add the red pepper (you can use any coloured pepper here. In fact, I once made a traffic light sandwich in class at high school; it was three colours of pepper between bread. Sounds a lot better than it was – who eats a raw pepper sandwich?) and carrot and cook for a further 5 minutes.

Add the lentils, paprika and herbs and stir it all up, then pour in the stock and simmer for 10 minutes or until the liquid has been absorbed. Whilst waiting you could listen to the full 8:42-minute version of Prince's 'Purple Rain' and rock out! Leave to cool for 20 minutes.

Meanwhile, preheat your oven to 180°C. Once the mixture has cooled, stir in the eggs and cheese and smash up the Crunchy Nut Clusters so they are no longer clusters, just bits really, Crunchy Nut bits. Add the bits into the mixture and stir it good. Press the mix into a foil-lined loaf tin and cover with more foil to make a lid. You need to cook this for 20 minutes, then remove the foil lid and cook for a further 20 minutes. All these 20 minutes of waiting time, what to do? Here are a few suggestions:

- Try to draw this without going over the same line twice or lifting your pen from the page.
- Make an origami paper finger game.
- Write down all the things you're going to enjoy about this nut roast.
- Draw a picture of Donald Duck from memory – unless you're a skilled artist the result will be nothing like Donald Duck, and probably hilarious.

Now it's ready. Take it out of the oven and let it rest for 5 minutes so you don't burn the roof of your mouth and get that annoying mouth blister that you constantly poke with your tongue!

The Shreddie Mix 2

1. 'Ducktales'
   John Griggs
2. 'Jump in the Line'
   Harry Belafonte
3. 'Hit Me With Your
   Best Shot'
   Pat Benatar

Ordinarily I would avoid Grape Nuts at all costs. When eating them with milk, it is kind of like eating broken glass. Not something I would recommend. These, along with porridge, are two 'cereals' I detest. I don't even think you can class porridge as cereal; the thought of it really turns my stomach, but, you know, each to their own!

So when it came to cooking with Grape Nuts I was very apprehensive. My face screwed up as I tried the first bite, but I have to say I was very surprised. The glassiness of the cereal disappeared as it soaked up the meat juices, and I was left chewing and smiling in delight. So please don't judge a cereal on first taste, and who knows, maybe some porridge with a bit of red meat in it might change my mind? But baby steps, eh?

MAKES 20 MEATBALLS
- 500g minced beef
- ½ onion, finely chopped
- 1 clove garlic, finely chopped
- 120g Grape Nuts (or you can use broken-up All Bran if you prefer), plus extra to garnish
- 2 tablespoons grated parmesan
- 1 egg, beaten
- Salt and freshly ground black pepper, to season
- A few fresh basil leaves, to garnish

For the sauce
- 2 x 400g cans chopped tomatoes
- 2 tablespoons tomato purée
- 1 tablespoon dried basil
- 2 cloves garlic, chopped

In a large mixing bowl, combine the beef, chopped onion and garlic, Grape Nuts, parmesan, egg and salt and pepper. This is where you get dirty – get stuck in with those hands to mix it all together (you could also use your feet and sell the video online, if you're into that sort of thing).

Once it's mixed, roll it into balls. I prefer 3cm balls, because this way I'll know they are cooked right through, and also I find balls bigger than that are quite hard to fit into your mouth.

Heat a frying pan on a medium-high heat and add some oil. Now cook dem balls for 5–10 minutes, continuously turning them so you don't burn them on the outside, until they are browned and cooked through.

Now let's get a bit saucy. Tip the chopped tomatoes, tomato purée, basil and garlic in a pan and bring to the boil, then simmer on a low heat for 5 minutes. Add a little salt and pepper to taste.

Serve the meatballs mixed through the beautiful sauce you have just concocted, garnished with a few Grape Nuts and basil leaves, or maybe with some spaghetti, dough balls and an episode of *Jersey Shore* for the true Italian experience.

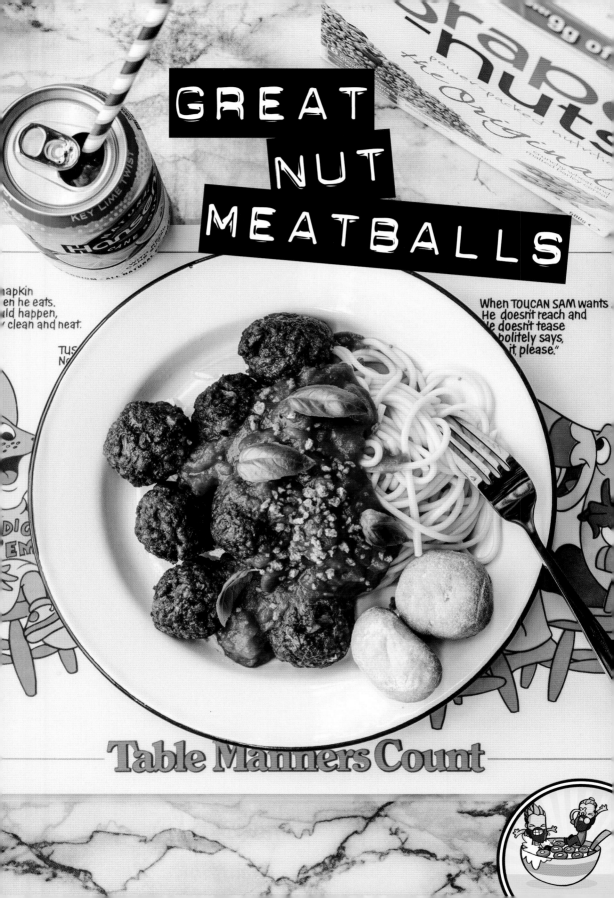

WHILE IT'S STILL CRISPY...

Ten Cereal Killer Café favourites are hidden in the word square below. See if you can find them all before your Weetabix goes soggy.

```
S E I P S I R K E C I R R V K
R Z O S U C R A M U E R A U F
W O R O D A U P U G M H L H S
D S U Z Z H M W I Q U O M Y A
G W B X I B A T E E W N O O N
W C M C L H E N H Y L E N L N
N O C G H H P U N H S Y D I A
S C N J T E R N J A A M M Z T
T O I Y C J E E N P H O I Z F
R P N L D I N R S I F N L Y M
A O S H R E D D I E S S K V J
T P G U R Q X A A O E T B R S
P S C M A R T I N F S E M T E
O X S W O L L A M H S R A M G
P H Q N E S J E Q I Z Q Z Y I
```

1. **POP TARTS**
2. **TONY THE TIGER**
3. **WEETABIX**
4. **COCO POPS**
5. **ALMOND MILK**
6. **RICE KRISPIES**
7. **MARSHMALLOWS**
8. **HONEY MONSTER**
9. **SHREDDIES**
10. **CHEERIOS**

TOP 5

WITTY COMEBACKS

1. You think you're hot shit, but you're just cold diarrhoea.
2. Talk to the hand 'cos the face ain't listening.
3. I know you are, but what am I?
4. Sphincter says what?
5. Don't push me, push a Push Pop.

TOP 5 QUALITY STREET

1. Green triangle
2. Caramel swirl
3. Orange chocolate crunch
4. Vanilla fudge
5. Strawberry delight

BIG MOUTH BILLY BASS

DO NOT PRESS
THE RED BUTTON

HOOPY HONEY KEESH WITH HI-AM

Quiche is popularised as a woman's food, but don't let that put you off; show your manliness by eating a slice of quiche Lorraine, whilst sipping on a glass of Lambrini, then nibble on a Kinder Bueno, just before getting your nails done.

Have you ever noticed that all yoghurt adverts are geared towards women, too? There are no yoghurts that have a grown man in the advert. None. I'd like to see a man's yoghurt on the market, just so I don't have to compromise my masculinity when buying a 6-pack of Müller corners.

Here the Cheerios make up the base of the quiche, and when preparing it, try not to drop it. (That's a pretty good joke right there. Where's my award?)

MAKES 1 QUICHE (FOR SHARING)

- 200g Honey Cheerios
- 6 eggs, beaten
- 25g melted butter
- 100ml double cream
- 100g hi-am (ham), chopped
- 100g cheddar cheese, grated
- Salt and freshly ground black pepper, to season

To start with, it's blender time. Blitz the Cheerios until they are dust, then tip out the powder into a mixing bowl. Add 1 beaten egg and the melted butter and mix with a Spoontula (This is a real thing that I haven't made up – it's a spoon/spatula hybrid, because how many times have you been stirring something with a spoon and thought 'I wish this spoon was a spatula'. Well, worry no more, get yourself a Spoontula!)

Once the pastry is ready, grease a round baking or flan tin approx. 22cm, and tightly shape the mix into a circle, you know, like a quiche. Pop this in the fridge for 15 minutes while you make the filling.

Preheat the oven to 150°C. Beat the rest of the eggs with the cream, and add the chopped ham and grated cheese, (when it comes to selecting cheese, whatever cheddar is on a discount offer usually works best) and season with salt and pepper. Pour the mix into the base and cook for 40–45 minutes.

Are you thinking what I'm thinking? 45 minutes is the perfect amount of time to watch an episode of Quantum Leap – the ones where he woke up as a woman were the best.

Remove the tray from the oven and let the keesh cool before eating. Serve with a side of Grazia magazine and a good dollop of office gossip.

'I'M NOT A SHRIMP, I'M A KING PRAWN. OK?!' If you're a Muppets fan, then you'll know what I'm talking about.

The Muppets is a childhood favourite that spans generations. But in hindsight, most of them suffered from some pretty bad character traits:

MISS PIGGY
morbid jealousy and body dysmorphia

GONZO
self-harm

FOZZIE BEAR
delusional

ANIMAL
feral (he wasn't a pet but was made to wear a collar and leash!)

STATLER AND WALDORF
misanthropy

But you just can't help but love them!

If you were lucky enough to grow up in the 80s you also had the Muppet Babies. I'm not sure if it was just me but, as you never saw the face of the nanny, only the ankles, I always pictured her looking like my mum!

2 SERVINGS
- 1 egg
- 100ml whole milk
- 100g plain flour
- Fistful of Crunchy Nut cornflakes approx. 20g
- Salt and freshly ground black pepper, to season
- ½ teaspoon hot paprika
- 200g cooked and peeled shrimp or prawns
- Store-bought honey and mustard dressing, to serve

First off, beat the egg and milk together in a cereal bowl and set aside.

In a second cereal bowl, sift in your flour.

Now crush the cornflakes – a rolling pin will be hard work, so you could pop them into a blender to save on precious energy. They need to be quite fine, like the consistency of rock salt. Place them in a third bowl along with the salt, pepper and paprika.

Here you can get a little train going. Roll your shrimp into the flour, then the eggy mixture, then into the Crunchy Nut mixture, and then deep-fry them in a pan for 10–20 seconds or until golden brown. You need to act quite fast and there's a lot of multitasking here, so try not to screw it up!

Scoop out the cooked shrimps using a slotted spoon and set on a plate lined with kitchen roll to drain, then serve immediately with the honey and mustard dressing as a dipping sauce. Mmmmmmmm.

HONEY

NUT

POPCORN SHRIMP

80

The Shreddie Mix

2

RICEOTTO KRISPIES

This one's for the true cereal lover – those of you who wake up in the morning and head straight to the cereal cupboard, and then again for lunch and dinner. But now at least you can cook a hearty meal and still get your cereal fix!

2 SERVINGS
- Knob of butter
- Glug olive oil
- 1 onion, finely chopped
- 2 cloves garlic, finely chopped
- 2 celery sticks, finely chopped
- 1 glass dry white wine
- 500ml chicken or vegetable stock
- 100g pancetta, chopped
- 100g mushrooms, diced
- 400g Rice Krispies
- 200ml double cream
- Salt and freshly ground black pepper, to taste
- Grated parmesan, to serve

Heat the butter and oil in a pan on a low heat, and add the chopped onion, garlic and celery. Cook until softened, then add the white wine and leave to simmer for 5 minutes. Heat the stock in a separate pan then add to the mix, keeping it simmering.

In a separate pan, fry the pancetta and mushrooms.

Add the Rice Krispies to the stock, stir in the cream, take off the heat and leave to absorb the flavours for 2 minutes. Mix in the pancetta and mushrooms, season, and serve immediately, scattered with parmesan.

SPOT THE DIFFERENCE

How many differences can you spot between these two photographs of yours truly? We'll give you the answer at the back of the book, or maybe we won't and you'll just have to keep looking...

First off, take that look off your face. I know what it sounds like, but this recipe is a game changer – it might seem bizarre and a bit WTF, but trust me, once you let this meaty crunchy sensation pass your lips you will never look at a Shredded Wheat in the same way again! Imagine a sausage roll but with a crunch you can hear across a crowded room. Gregg would be mega jelly.

This recipe does require a steady hand, because the Shredded Wheat biscuits need a little landscaping, so have a few extra on hand in case of a wheat biscuit catastrophe!

MAKES 8
- 8 Shredded Wheat biscuits
- 1 medium red onion
- 400g sausage meat
- 100g cheddar, grated
- Salt and freshly ground black pepper, to season
- 2 eggs, beaten (listening to Michael Jackson's 'Beat It' while beating eggs is a must)

The Shreddie Mix 2

8. 'Ready to Go'
   Republica
9. 'Drinking in LA'
   Bran Van 3000
10. 'Song For Whoever'
    The Beautiful South

First, preheat your oven to 180°C.

Take your Shredded Wheat biscuits and a butter knife, and if you peer in the end of a biscuit you can tell there is some room down there, so gently poke the knife in, creating a hollow middle to the centre and flip it round. Repeat with each biscuit. Remember, a Shredded Wheat biscuit isn't made of steel, so don't jab jab jab, be gentle like you are playing Operation. You'll see the join on each side of the biscuit, these are easily separated with a knife, just slide down and split the biscuit open and score off any sticky out bits of wheat to leave two tidy shells ready to be filled with the meaty goodness.

You now need to chop your onions (life hack: chew gum while chopping onions to avoid teary eyes) and fry 'em. Easy. Then put your sausage meat, cooked onions, grated cheese, salt and pepper into a large mixing bowl and, if you're like me and don't like touching raw meat with your hands, use a Spoontula (I promise I'm not sponsored by the Spoontula inventor, they are just amazing!). Mix all the ingredients well and divide into eight equal amounts.

Next, grease a baking tray and lay out the Shredded Wheat biscuits. You'll notice that one half of the biscuit is a little thicker than the other: this will be the base. Fill each biscuit base with the sausage meat mixture, spreading it out evenly. The lids are ready to go on now, so you need to get a pastry brush and generously brush all the exposed wheat with the beaten egg.

Now you can relax for 20 minutes while they bake in the oven. Make yourself a brew, walk your dog, do facial yoga – basically, there are loads of ways to spend 20 minutes, so I'll leave that bit up to you.

When they are ready, you'll know from the smell, serve piping hot, maybe with a dollop of ketchup, but I'm not your real dad, so choose your own condiment.

SHREDDED SAUSAGE WHEATS

Or shreddage rolls!!

WHEATY CRUSTED SALMON

Growing up, there were a few staple meals in our house. Fish fingers, which I'm sure back then used the term 'fish' very loosely. Then there were Findus Crispy Pancakes. Now, if you haven't had one of these delights before, I'll explain. It's a frozen savoury pancake which has been folded in half with a minced beef filling and coated in something nondescript and crispy. I'm not sure exactly why these were so popular in the 90s, but I can honestly say I will never again let one of these pass my lips as long as I live!

2 SERVINGS
- 1 Shredded Wheat biscuit
- 3 tablespoons grated parmesan
- 3 tablespoons pesto
- 2 salmon fillets approx. 240g, skin on

First things first, preheat the oven to 180°C.

Now you need to crush that Shredded Wheat – hammer the life out of it with a rolling pin and tip it into your mixing bowl. Add the parmesan and pesto and mix well.

Now place your delicious salmon fillets on a greased baking tray and spread the mix over the top side (not the skin side, obvs!).

Bake the salmon in the oven for 15 minutes, and serve with salad, or potatoes – or my choice would be a potato waffle.

Beans, beans, the musical fruit, the more you eat, the more likely you are to experience abdominal cramping, diarrhoea and extreme flatulence.

These bean bombs really are 'da bomb', which is a totally dated cultural slang term which, if used in a modern-day setting, would make you a social outcast. Other terms to avoid are:

TERM	USED IN A SENTENCE
'NOT'	'This Sunny D is totally good for you, NOT.'
'Talk to the hand'	'Ricky Martin is definitely not gay.' 'Talk to the hand, beeotch.'
'Fly'	'Your shell suit is so fly.'
'Then why don't you marry it?'	'I love my new Rachel cut.' 'Then why don't you marry it?'
'Bogus'	'This millennium bug is totally bogus.'
'Get a life'	'I'm just going to Blockbuster to pick up the new Julia Roberts movie.' 'Get a life.'

MAKES 20 BOMBS

- 200g Shreddies
- 2 eggs
- Vegetable oil, for frying
- ½ x 400g can of kidney beans, drained
- ½ x 400g can of butter beans, drained
- ½ x 400g can of black beans, drained
- 1 x 400g can chickpeas, drained
- 1 x 435g can refried beans
- 2 tablespoons chilli paste
- 2 tablespoons garlic paste
- Salt and freshly ground black pepper, to season

Get prepped first: blitz the Shreddies in a blender until they are fine like sugar, and separate out three-quarters of these for the mixture, setting aside the remainder for the coating. Next, beat the eggs and set aside in a small bowl – a cereal bowl works perfectly. Get a frying pan ready and fill it about 3cm deep with oil, ready for shallow frying the bean bombs.

Get your trusty mixing bowl at the ready – now you can either pulse the beans and chickpeas in a blender to break them up, or down (breaking them up or down, although opposite, are essentially the same thing, right?). Alternatively, you can fire them all into your bowl and mash them up (but you can't mash them down. Weird.). Then, add the refried beans to the pulsed mixture and give it all a good stir.

Add the larger amount of the blitzed Shreddies to the bowl, along with the refried beans, chilli, garlic, salt and pepper to taste, and half the beaten egg and mix everything together with a Spoontula, or your hands if you're feeling dirty. Roll the bean concoction into 5cm-wide balls, about the size of a bouncy ball that is also 5cm wide.

Next, coat the balls in the remaining beaten egg, roll them generously in the blitzed Shreddies in the bowl, and pop into the frying pan to cook, turning regularly, for 5 minutes or until golden brown.

I like to take them off and let them sit on a piece of kitchen roll, to pretend the absorbent sheet will soak up the majority of the calories, leaving me with a healthy snack (but I'm not even kidding myself with this one!). Now get ready to be bombed!

BEAN
BOMBS

MIXED-UP WORDS

We're always mixing cereals and mixing cereal cocktails in the Cereal Killer Café – it's a mixed-up kind of place. The kind of place where you can eat cereal all day is always going to be a bit mixed-up and that's the way we like it.

Sometimes, we even get our words muxed ip. See if you can work out some Cereal Killer Café favourites from the mixed up words below.

SCUM COOT POOH

PROOF I SLUT

HOG IN TINKLE

CANCAN SPARKED PLOP

MCCOCA HOLE KILT

DICK SHAG BABE PACT

HE WEDDED TRASH

MY CLUCK RASH

CHECK NO CURLY NUN FARTS

CLOGS LICKER LIES

TOP 5

SONG

LYRICS

1. 'Like a tramp in the night I was begging for you'

2. 'I'd rather have a piece of toast, watch the evening news'

3. 'Lucky that my breasts are small and humble, so you don't confuse them with mountains'

4. 'What about the elephants, have we lost their trust?'

5. 'I'm as serious as cancer'

Now turn the book, or stand on your head, to see where they came from!

The Songs…
1. 'Touch Me (I Want Your Body)', Samantha Fox, 1986
2. 'Life', Des'ree, 1998
3. 'Whenever, Wherever', Shakira, 2002
4. 'Earth Song', Michael Jackson, 1995
5. 'Rhythm Is A Dancer', Snap!, 1992

CHILLI PARTYMIX

There ain't no party like an S Club party. Get this party started on a Saturday night. We like to party, we like, we like to party. Tonight we're going to party like it's 1999. I could name many more songs with party in the title, but I think you're in a party spirit by now, and what your party needs (apart from the obvious S Club 7 song) is a huge bowl of Shreddies party mix! You've got all the textures you need here: the crispy crunch of the Shreddie, the fluffiness of the popcorn, the smooth break of a cheese biscuit, and the crunchy snap in a peanut. Om nom nom nom.

So your party is in full flow, S Club 7 are blasting out of your boom box, everyone is complimenting you on the surprisingly delicious party mix, but what games are you going to entertain your guests with?

Yeah, you could go with playing charades or Pictionary – boring! So why not go wild and play strip Twister/eat a banana through a pair of tights/who can deep-throat a courgette the furthest/who is the quickest person to peel a banana with their feet.

MAKES SHIT LOADS

- 1 bag microwaveable butter popcorn
- 35g parmesan
- 1 teaspoon hot chilli powder
- 1 teaspoon garlic powder
- 5 tablespoons olive oil
- 200g Shreddies
- 100g cheese mix biscuits
- 140g dry roasted peanuts

Get that oven fired up to 180°C and pop the corn in the microwave as per the packet instructions.

While your corn's a poppin', finely grate the parmesan and mix it with the chilli and garlic powders.

Now get your trusty large mixing bowl and chuck in the popcorn with all of the remaining party ingredients. Slowly drizzle the oil over your mix while stirring it – a third hand is usually quite helpful at this point, but if you're making this alone, then get creative! Stir and stir until all of the mix is coated with the flavours. Now slowly sprinkle over the cheese and spice seasoning whilst stirring continuously.

Now that the mix is coated, it's ready to go in the oven. TBH, you'll probably need two baking trays for this, so spread out the mix evenly and pop it in the oven for 15–20 minutes.

When finished, let the mix cool completely and serve in a jazzy bowl or cereal box – I'll let you decide on that one.

SMASH HITS

Cereal Killer Diner

After a long day pouring cereal (or proofreading erotic fiction, or however you pay your bills), I'm sure the last thing you want to do is stand in front of a stove, prodding potatoes as they bob around in a pot of bubbling water. But if you still want to impress your best frenemy with your adventurous culinary skills, this is the recipe for you. It can be prepped in less than 10 minutes, which means more time watching re-runs of Friends.

MAKES 2 BURGERS

- ¼ onion, roughly chopped
- ¼ sweet red pepper, deseeded and roughly chopped
- 2 cloves garlic (or 2 teaspoons of garlic paste, if you're lazy and need more time to watch Friends)
- 50g frozen peas
- ½ x 400g can chickpeas, drained
- 1 tablespoon hot paprika
- 2 tablespoons tomato purée
- 1 teaspoon chilli paste
- 2 egg whites
- Salt and freshly ground black pepper, to season
- 1 teaspoon mixed dried herbs
- 4 Weetabix
- Vegetable oil, for frying
- Fancy bun and any of your preferred condiments, to serve

Pile all the ingredients into your blender, except the Weetabix, and blend until well mixed but not a paste.

Now wash your paws, we don't know where those hands have been! Get a big mixing bowl and unwrap your Weetabix and, like a true gladiator, crush the biscuits with your bare hands – try it one-handed, try both hands; quite a nice feeling, eh?

Now chuck the blended mix into the Weetabix and get your hands in the bowl and start mixing it up. Don't be afraid to smush it in between your fingers, just try not to get it in your hair! Leave it to one side for 10 minutes.

Heat some oil in a pan on a high heat and make the burger mix into two patty shapes that SpongeBob would be proud of. Fry each patty for 3–5 minutes on both sides until golden brown.

Serve straightaway in a fancy bun, with your choice of dressing. I'm partial to a bit of crushed avocado, peanut butter and hot sauce, but you know, horses for courses. Now kick back with some friends and Friends, and see if Rachel and Ross are on, or off, or ON A BREAK!

BRANFRIES

As an Irish person I do live up to the stereotype of a potato-loving Paddy, and you know what? I love it. There is no shame in loving the potato. Potato bread, chips, crisps, rosti, hash, boiled, sautéed, fried, steamed, raw – it's all heaven. Mashed potato even makes a great dip for crisps, just sayin'... Now, Bran Flake chips, or, if you're in a hurry and like to shorten words, branfries, are beautiful chips with a crunchy coating. What's not to love?!

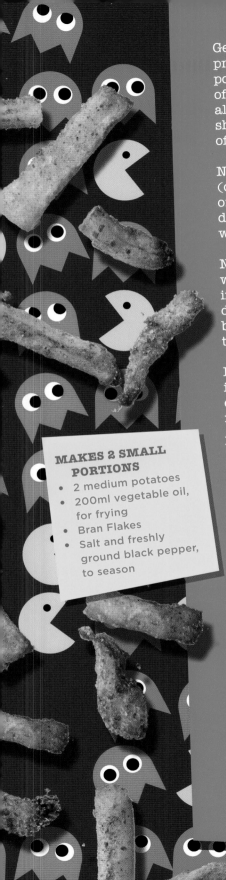

Get your potatoes and get them peeled. This is probably the most boring job in the world, and potato skin is very aerodynamic, as when it flies off the potato it never seems to land in the sink, always around it! Now cut the potatoes into chip shapes – not too thick – then parboil them in a pan of salted boiling water, drain, then put to one side.

Now heat up the oil. You can use a deep-fat fryer (does anyone still have one of these?) or just shallow-fry the chips in a pan (the deeper the better) and turn them repeatedly while cooking.

Next, tip your Bran Flakes into a sandwich bag with some salt and pepper, grab a rolling pin, or, if you're like me, an empty wine bottle usually does this job, and start rolling the Bran Flakes to break them down. They need to be very fine (like the consistency of salt, or sugar, or molly).

I'm not gonna lie, it isn't the easiest of jobs, but it's a good workout for the arms. Make these every night and you'll look like Popeye in a few weeks – less the tattoos and anger issues. Another option is chucking them into a blender, but there's something a lot more satisfying about smashing them down with your bare hands/a wine bottle!

Now, throw the chips into the bag and shake it like a Polaroid picture (NB: never shake a Polaroid picture, this is a terrible habit that can ruin your picture quality, and we can blame Mr Outkast for that one...).

You're ready to get your fry on! Your chips should be well covered, so gently lower them into the oil – I say gently because hot oil hurts when splashed on bare skin, d'uh! Now keep turning those bad boys until they are golden brown and bloody delicious looking, then scoop them out and put them onto a some kitchen roll to absorb the extra oil.

You've got your branfries now, so you can eat them however you want: on their own, with a burger, as a topping on a pizza (this is an actual thing in Belfast), but one thing's for sure, you'll probably never want to eat a boring normal chip again!

MAKES 2 SMALL PORTIONS
- 2 medium potatoes
- 200ml vegetable oil, for frying
- Bran Flakes
- Salt and freshly ground black pepper, to season

The History

It's no shock that we are a nation of cereal lovers – I mean, you're reading a book about cooking with the stuff, for Pete's sake! But have you ever wondered why the hell the country's obsession came to reach such a frantic, milky boiling point? Well, the following story is completely true and not made-up at all.

Let me take you back in time, to a land free from internet, Twitter and Kerry Katona. The year is 1863, in North America, and there was some weird shit happening amongst these God-fearing Americans. First of all, how about their breakfast of choice? Pork, beef and coffee, and we're talking pork chops and beef joints here, washed down with some whiskey. As you can imagine, such a diet, so lacking in fibre, was causing havoc on the tummies of the nation. Luckily enough, toilet roll had just been invented a few years earlier, so, you know, every cloud...

Now, ask any goody-goody God-lover of this time, and you were sure to be told that constipation was a punishment for eating God's animals and, what's more, a meaty meal fuelled lust and laziness! A few devout Christians worked tirelessly to solve this crisis, and Dr James Caleb Jackson invented the first version of cereal. He called it Granula. These tasteless, tooth-smashing bricks had to be soaked overnight just to make them chewable. Yum – sign me up! Despite this, they were a hit.

DR KELLOGG

Meanwhile, in his Michigan retreat, health guru Dr John Harvey Kellogg was treating the rich and famous with some rather bizarre procedures. Bear in mind that Dr Kellogg, being a devout Christian, fully believed that a healthy body meant a healthy mind and, of course, a healthy mind was one free from any kind of naughty sexual thoughts. Dr Kellogg himself was a virgin till the day he died, never consummating his marriage and even adopting all of his children. Now that's dedication.

But back to the good doctor's bizarre therapies. One of them involved a yoghurt enema that cleaned out your bowels, with 50 per cent of the yoghurt taken orally, and the other 50 per cent administered... ahem... anally! Mind you, if you ask any confirmed carnivore to consume about a gallon of yoghurt, that's probably what they'll tell you to do with it, anyway.

Now, when Dr Kellogg heard what Dr JC Jackson was doing with his breakfast bricks, he thought, 'I can do that better,' and made something a little more palatable. But when JC heard about this copy cat, he was all, 'Bitch, please!' and slapped a lawsuit on Kellogg. This lead to a huge one-letter change in the name, and Granola was born!

CONTINUED ON PAGE 118

SWEET STUFF

THREE FACTS THAT NO ONE KNOWS ABOUT THE CEREAL KILLER TWINS:

▶ **We were champion figure skaters when we were eight years old.**
▶ **We can breathe through our eyes.**
▶ **We love banoffee almost as much as we love cereal.**

So when we married two of our loves, you can imagine the excitement.

MAKES 1 WHOLE PIE

- 250g Toffee Crisp cereal
- 200g unsalted butter
- 100g dark brown soft sugar
- 397g can condensed milk
- 3 bananas, sliced
- Can of squirty cream

The Lucky Charm Mix
STEREO
A
C-60

1. 'Where Everybody Knows Your Name (Cheers theme)' Gary Portnoy

2. 'Man in the Mirror' Michael Jackson

3. 'We Didn't Start The Fire' Billy Joel

4. 'Steal My Sunshine' Len

First, blend the cereal until it's nice and fine, then melt 100g of the butter and mix it into the cereal until all the grains are coated. Now spoon the mix into the bottom of a greased 20cm round cake tin, and press it down evenly, making a little lip up the sides to keep all the caramel in. Pop this in the fridge for 30 minutes to set while you make the filling.

Melt the remaining butter in a pan on a low heat with the sugar, stirring, until the sugar is dissolved. Pour in the condensed milk and turn the heat up. Cook this for about a minute while constantly stirring and – BINGO – you've got yourself some caramel.

Pour the caramel over the crispy base and pop the tin back in the fridge to get its chill on for about an hour.

I find it better to dress the banoffee crisp with bananas and cream just before serving – unless you plan on eating the whole pie in one go, in which case generously layer the banana over the set caramel and smother with cream. Beautiful!

BANOFFEE CRISP

The good old Coco Pop, a cereal known and loved by many. The 'I'd rather have a bowl of Coco Pops' song is now stuck in your head, and probably will be for the rest of the day. You're welcome, but it could be worse, it could be 'Cotton-Eye Joe'!

And if like me you remember the 'Rednex' from 'Cotton-Eye Joe' fame, it makes you wonder what was going on in the 90s if this song was a No. 1 smash hit. Yes, the song is pretty damn catchy, but the band dressed up as rednecks, who are the American lower-class dregs of society. It's the equivalent of a band called 'Chavs' dressed in tracksuits and Burberry caps selling music in America. Actually, that was East 17, wasn't it?!

*bonus points if you can remember the words to 'Old pop in an oak'.

Now, this is a bit of a layer cake – the crunchiness of the Coco Pops base with the gooeyness of the brownie sandwiched on top is some next-level s**t!

SERVES UP TO 8

- 250g milk chocolate
- 275g unsalted butter
- 3 eggs
- 275g caster sugar
- 100g plain flour
- 40g cocoa powder
- 6 Mars Bars
- 150g Coco Pops

Preheat the oven to 180°C. It's bain marie time! Melt the chocolate and 200g of the butter in a bain marie, then leave to cool to the temperature of a cucumber.

Next, break the eggs into a large mixing bowl – try not to get any eggshell in there, but if you do it might just add extra texture to the finished product. Add the sugar and whisk with an electric mixer until the mixture looks thick and creamy – like thick cream.

Now, pour the chocolate mixture into the bowl and mix together, then sift the flour and cocoa powder into the egg and sugar mixture and mix it up again. Line a shallow rectangular 28cm baking tin with greaseproof paper and scoop the mixture into it. Jam the tray into the oven and bake for 25 minutes.

Take the tray out of the oven and leave it to sit for 5 minutes, then tip it out onto one of those wire racks – or if you don't have one, use your dish drainer.

Now for the Coco Pops layer! Melt the remaining butter and the Mars Bars together in a bain marie, stirring as they melt – you could probably even use the same bain marie you did before, unless you've been really organised and washed it.

Then stir in your Coco Pops and mix them round thoroughly to coat in the Mars Bar mixture. Put the mix in the same baking tray (greaseproof lined, obviously) that you used for the brownie so the layers are the same size, and stick in the fridge to set.

Once both layers are cool, place the brownie on top of the Coco Pop mix and cut into squares. Now bask in the chocolicious, crunchy, chewy, melty, sticky, crispy, creamy, flaky orgasm-inducing traybake you have just created.

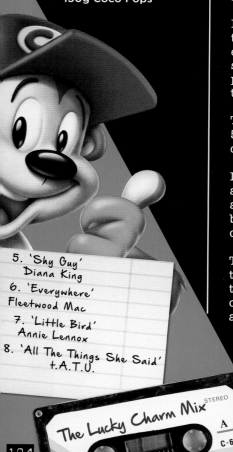

5. 'Shy Guy'
Diana King

6. 'Everywhere'
Fleetwood Mac

7. 'Little Bird'
Annie Lennox

8. 'All The Things She Said'
t.A.T.U.

The Lucky Charm Mix STEREO

A

C-60

COCO TOP BROWNIE

CURIOUSLY APPLE AND CINNAMON CRUMBLE

Apple crumble is a British classic. It's up there with a cup 'a' tea, queuing and a curry house.

I'm sure a lot of you did H.E. in high school or, for those who didn't, H.E. is Home Economics; it's like a subject that stuck through generations from the 50s, teaching you how to be a great housewife.

I remember a few things from H.E., but the only thing that I learnt and that I still practise today is the order in which you wash your dishes: glasses-mugs-plates/bowls-cutlery-pots/pans. This information is useless to kids these days; it's now put dishes in the dishwasher/take dishes out of the dishwasher.

I know every generation thinks the generation after them sucked, but future generations really are screwed, as they have grown up without knowing the following:

- They will never know the fear of calling your crush's house and hoping their parents don't answer.
- Setting your video recorder to record your favourite show and just hoping to god no one changes the channel!
- Recording songs off the radio and getting furious when the presenter talks over the end of the song.
- Rewinding a tape with a pencil.
- The modem dial-up tune.
- Only having four TV channels.
- Blowing into a computer cartridge.
- Wanting to be gunged.

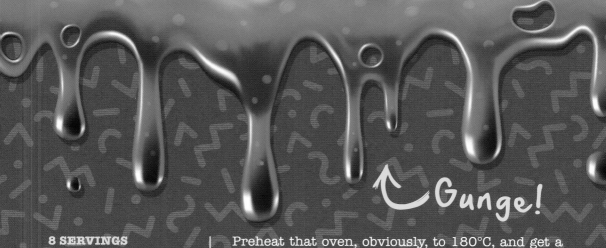

↶ Gunge!

8 SERVINGS

- 900g Bramley apples, cored, peeled and sliced
- 1 teaspoon ground cinnamon
- 2 tablespoons water
- 125g dark soft brown sugar
- 225g plain flour
- 75g unsalted butter
- 100g Curiously Cinnamon

Preheat that oven, obviously, to 180°C, and get a large shallow baking dish ready.

Pop the apples, cinnamon, water and 25g of the sugar in a saucepan and cook over a low heat until the apples are soft. Spoon into the baking dish, and now you're ready to start the crumble.

Sift the flour into your ever-important large mixing bowl, then add the butter and remaining sugar. Now wash your hands, because you're about to get dirty – unless, of course, you think that whoever is eating this needs to build up their immune system, in which case prepare the crumble with dirty hands. (Gary used to eat chewing gum off the ground when he was younger, and as a result he has such a strong immune system that he never gets sick, like, ever!)

So, get your hands into the bowl and start to blend the butter into the flour with your fingertips until the mixture resembles breadcrumbs. Now smash your Curiously Cinnamon – not too much, but you want all the bits to be broken – then add it to the crumble mixture and stir through.

Scatter the crumble over the top of the apples and spread it out real nice and even. Pop the dish into the oven for 30–40 minutes, until golden and bubbling, then serve with custard, or ice cream, or ice cream and custard and cream and more custard...

9. 'Summer of '69'
Bryan Adams

10. 'Things Can Only Get Better'
D:Ream

11. 'Justified and Ancient'
People of 'K' Feat. Crystal

12. 'Virtual Insanity'
Jamiroquai

GOLDIE NUGG GAZILLIONNAIRE

Golden Nuggets, or, as we like to call them, 'goldie nug nugs', are not made from real gold, just as millionaire's shortbread is not made exclusively for millionaires. Foods can be pretty confusing, eh?

Pineapple is not made from pines, nor apples.
Coconuts are not made of coco.
Fish fingers are not made from fishes' fingers.
Hamburgers have no ham in them.
Shepherd's pie is not made from shepherds.
KFC has zero chicken in it.

12 SERVINGS
- 100g unsalted butter
- 3 Mars Bars, chopped up
- 200g Golden Nuggets
- 200g cooking milk chocolate

For the caramel
- 100g unsalted butter
- 100g dark soft brown sugar
- 1 x 397g tin condensed milk

All right. Firstly, melt the butter in a pan on a low heat with the chopped-up Mars Bars. The Mars Bars here give the millionaire's shortbread a new dimension – well on top of the other new dimension you'll create with the cereal!

Now, blitz up the Golden Nuggets in your good old food processor, and add the melted goo to the golden nug nug dust. Give this all a good mix together.

Next, line a medium-sized baking tray (approx. 28cm x 18cm) with greaseproof paper and spread out your nug nug mixture evenly, and press it firmly into shape. Hell, you might want to use this book and your body weight! Pop this into the fridge to set for 30 minutes, and now make caramel.

You'll have to melt the butter and sugar in a pan on a low heat, and make sure you keep on stirring until the sugar has dissolved. Add the condensed milk and bring up to the boil pretty snappy. And don't forget to keep on stirring until you've got a caramelly pot of tastiness. Now spread this on top of the nug nug base and leave to set for an hour.

When that's all done, you'll wanna melt the chocolate in a bain marie – a heatproof bowl set over a pan of simmering water. Let it cool slightly, then take out the chilled cereal and caramel base, then the chocolate – obviously.

While the three tiers of perfection are cooling in the fridge for 2 hours, feel free to lick both the condensed caramel pan and the chocolate bowl. Go on, I won't judge you.

The Honey Monster is a British icon. He has grown from an odd-looking, genuinely creepy monster in the 70s – 'tell 'em about the honey, Mummy' haunted my childhood dreams – to a cuddly, playful, yellow, fluffy thing that is as cute as a button; a makeover that Madonna would be jealous of. The recent change in the cereal's name from Sugar Puffs to Honey Monster Puffs has reinforced the fact that sugar is clearly the worst word ever in the cereal business!

These Honey Monster rice cakes are a fun and simple appetiser or snack on the go, or, if you are unlucky enough to have kids, making these will keep them entertained in between drawing on the walls and singing 'that' song from the latest Disney movie!

MAKES 6ish CAKES
- 200g Sugar Puffs – sorry, Honey Monster puffs
- 1 jar of Nutella
- 1 jar of peanut butter

The Lucky Charm Mix STEREO
A
C-60

To say this is a simple recipe is an understatement, I mean, just look at the ingredients! So get a baking sheet – the bigger the baking sheet the more cakes you'll get (but make sure it's bigger than this book) and line it with greaseproof paper. Have another separate sheet ready to cover the cakes.

Next, measure out your Sugar Honey Monster Puffs (will this new name stick?) – you'll want the cakes to be about 5cm deep and about 10cm in diameter when you cut them out. Tip the cereal into a large mixing bowl and lightly bash it with the end of a rolling pin – you are just wanting to break them down slightly, not too much.

Now to the microwave (insert joke about a mouse waving here). Pop the mixing bowl in and cook on high for 2 minutes, but take it out and stir the mixture every 30 seconds to stop the puffs from burning. You'll notice them getting quite sticky; this is perfect.

Now, you gotta act fast here – you are against the clock when the microwave goes 'ding'. Pop the puffs back into the baking tin, level out, and cover with the greaseproof paper, then close this book and put it on top of the covered puffs. Place the book on the floor and stand on it – probably not the most conventional way of pressing them, but we found it the best method for getting enough pressure onto them so they are nice and dense.

Next, and again there is no time to dilly dally here, get a cookie cutter (circle ones look best, but you can always slice into squares for less wastage) and cut out your perfect little rice cakes. You need to act fast because when the honey dries, the cakes become rather brittle.

Now whack the cakes on a plate, smother some with Nutella, some with peanut butter, and even go wild with some Nutella and peanut butter mixes! Quick and simple, eh?

YELLOW MONSTER RICE CAKES

ALAN

CKC MASKS

By now you're probably thinking, 'Jeez, this book is brilliant. I just wish that I could look as cool as Alan and Gary ...' Well, that's not easy. Growing the beard takes ages and facial hair can get sweaty and itchy, and even a bit smelly when it collects little morsels of food. And it's just as bad for men. To save you the trouble, why not cut out these amazing face masks instead?

GARY

Careful with the holes by the ears where you will have to attach some string or an elastic band. You can strengthen those areas with a bit of sticky tape on the back. If you don't want to cut up your book, just photocopy them or scan 'em and print 'em. Make enough for all your friends and you can have a CKC party with dozens of us and CKC drinks and eats!

LUCKY LEPRECHAUN CHEESECAKE

Good ol' Lucky Charms – a lot of us remember this cereal from our childhood, but it's another 90s favourite where someone thought, 'this cereal is too nice for British people, let's ban it'. But the marshmallowy goodness is still available in America (and the Cereal Killer Café, of course), so getting your hands on this cereal isn't impossible.

Although you'll be paying a little extra for this imported delight than you would for your normal cereal, this isn't a normal cereal – it's got freeze-dried freakin' marshmallows in it! To educate anyone who hasn't experienced a freeze-dried marshmallow before, it's basically the best thing to ever happen to cereal, because a Lucky Charm without marshmallows is a bloody unlucky charm.

And for the record, leprechauns should always be thought of as happy little mites looking for a pot of gold, so the horror movie franchise version of the leprechaun is basically slandering the whole legend of our beloved little friends. Just look at the movie titles:

Leprechaun (OK)
Leprechaun 2 (didn't think it needed a sequel, but fine)
Leprechaun 3 (really? Who is paying for this?)
Leprechaun 4: In Space (what?? I don't... how the?!)
Leprechaun in the Hood (the hood? The goddamn hood!
What are you smoking?!)
Leprechaun Back 2 tha Hood (why did he go back?
And what's with the slang, I might go cry into some
Lucky Charms now...)

**MAKES ONE
8-SLICE CHEESECAKE**
- 85g unsalted butter
- 140g Lucky Charms (separate out the marshmallows for the filling)
- 3 x 300g pots Philadelphia cream cheese
- 250g caster sugar
- 3 tablespoons plain flour
- 1 ½ teaspoons vanilla extract
- pinch of salt
- 3 large eggs, plus 1 more yolk
- 284ml carton soured cream
- Marshmallows and whipped double cream, to serve

Melt the butter in a medium pan, and meanwhile blend the cereal in a food processor until fine. Stir the cereal into the melted butter and press the mixture into a 5cm deep cake tin, about 22cm wide, evenly spreading it out to line the base of the tin. Put it in the fridge to set while you make the filling.

Beat the cream cheese with an electric mixer until smooth, gradually add the sugar, then the flour, vanilla extract and a pinch of salt. Whisk in the eggs and the yolk, one at a time, until combined. Then whisk in the soured cream. Finally, add the reserved Lucky Charms marshmallows, stirring to mix them through.

Preheat the oven to 200°C. Remove the tin from the fridge and spoon the filling over the cereal base until even. Bake for 10 minutes, then reduce the oven temperature to 90°C and bake for a further 25 minutes. Turn off the oven and leave the tin in the oven to cool for 2 hours.

Serve the cheesecake with peaks of whipped double cream around the edges, and a few extra Lucky Charms marshmallows on top of the cream, to – you know – make it look fancy.

Everybody loves a homemade cookie. It's probably one of the first things you properly baked with your mum when you were younger, and if you had brothers and sisters there were probably fights over who got to lick the bowl!

In our house as kids, we also used to have a real obsession with Garbage Pail Kids stickers. For those who aren't familiar, GPK stickers were collectable cards that featured gross characters with funny names. At the age of eight it was pretty hilarious to see a cartoon covered in snot (Leaky Lindsay) or a transsexual baby (Swell Mel) or a baby picking and eating his scab-covered body (Scabby Abby). It's a shame the whole world has gone PC on us, because you just don't get stuff like this any more.

MAKES 20 COOKIES

- 175g unsalted butter, softened, plus extra for greasing
- 200g soft dark brown sugar
- 100g caster sugar
- 1 egg and 1 yolk
- 200g plain flour
- ½ teaspoon bicarbonate of soda
- ½ teaspoon salt
- 60g Lucky Charms marshmallows

First off you'll need to preheat the oven to 170°C and line a baking sheet with greaseproof paper. Now, cream your butter and both kinds of sugar in a large mixing bowl. (Creaming is basically a fancy cooking term for mixing together.) Add the egg and egg yolk and beat until the mixture is as smooth as a freshly shaven bikini line. Next, sift in the flour with the bicarbonate of soda and salt, and mix until as smooth as a dolphin. Stir in the Lucky Charms marshmallows with a spoon.

Each cookie should be made from 1 heaped tablespoon of dough, because you want a nice big cookie. Shape the mixture onto the lined baking sheet, leaving space between the cookies, and bake for 10 minutes (in batches). Leave them to cool on the baking sheet for 5 minutes, then transfer to a wire rack to cool completely, or eat them straight away – just don't burn your mouth.

LUCKY LEPRECHAUN COOKIES

The popularity of Granola led Kellogg to experiment with other grains, and soon came a thin wheatmeal cracker. Just like in every place of work, there's always one lazy dick that does as little as possible, and Dr Kellogg's kitchen was no different. But this one lazy dick struck it lucky when he finished work for the night, leaving a job half done. He left out a sheet of wheatmeal cracker and, of course, it went stale! Upon arrival the next day, the stale wheatmeal sheet was put through the press, and out came flakes! That's right, that lazy dick hit the jackpot!

Kellogg's new flakes were a mega hit and swamped the nation like a Paris Hilton sex tape. People flocked to Kellogg's retreats to taste his flakes, and while being treated for his second nervous breakdown, Charles William Post thought 'I can do that better,' and that's where Grape Nuts came from. The glass-like, enamel-shattering Grape Nuts came with something that would shape all cereals for the future – advertising! Grape Nuts claimed in their ads that they could cure appendicitis, make red blood redder, and even fix wobbly teeth. And Americans lapped it up.

There were soon 107 brands of breakfast flakes, all selling the same thing, but using different advertising techniques. Kellogg's stayed ahead of the game with a bit of sexism. 'Wink at your greengrocer and get a free box of Cornflakes,' they said, which would nowadays be translated as, 'You're a slut, here's some cereal.'

The next game-changer came when the makers of Force cereal put a dapper cartoon man on the box. This lanky streak of piss was the first cereal box character, and his popularity was mega – he was the Harry Styles of his day. Other cereal companies were quick to

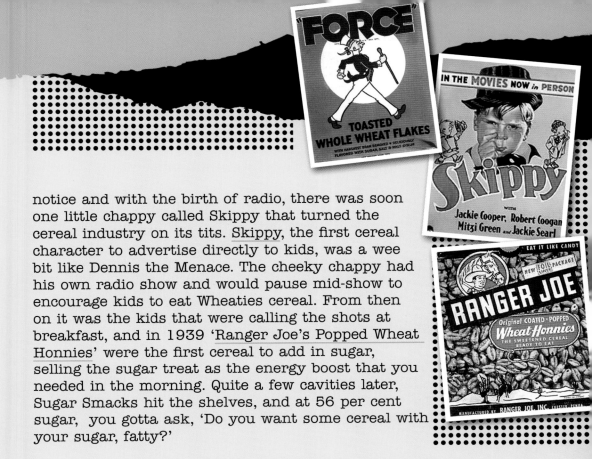

notice and with the birth of radio, there was soon one little chappy called Skippy that turned the cereal industry on its tits. Skippy, the first cereal character to advertise directly to kids, was a wee bit like Dennis the Menace. The cheeky chappy had his own radio show and would pause mid-show to encourage kids to eat Wheaties cereal. From then on it was the kids that were calling the shots at breakfast, and in 1939 'Ranger Joe's Popped Wheat Honnies' were the first cereal to add in sugar, selling the sugar treat as the energy boost that you needed in the morning. Quite a few cavities later, Sugar Smacks hit the shelves, and at 56 per cent sugar, you gotta ask, 'Do you want some cereal with your sugar, fatty?'

By the 1960s, 90 per cent of cereal was marketed towards children: the Lone Ranger, Yogi Bear, Dick Tracy and Fred Flintstone all became popular cartoons because they sold a ton of cereal. They were selling so much cereal through their cartoons that the law people shut them down, making it illegal to advertise to kids via cartoons – party poopers! But what came after was Tony, Snap Crackle and Pop, Coco... all the cereal characters we know today.

I'm sure if we could ask Dr John Harvey Kellogg what he thought of this empire he kicked off, he would probably run straight for a tub of yoghurt and stuff it into every orifice he had to rid himself of guilt about the monster he created. Oh, well, John, soz.

NO
BAKE
CLUSTER
CAKE

Chocolate and cereal are BFFs, and in this relationship it's always the cereal taking the lead role, with the chocolate being the side-kick. Kind of a Wayne/Garth thing; we all knew Garth was much better than Wayne, but Wayne never really let Garth shine, it was all Wayne's world, Wayne's world, party time, excellent. But what about Garth's world? I'm sure it's pretty excellent, too, and depending on opinion, possibly better than Wayne's world!

These cakes are so melt-in-your-mouth chocolatey, they'll satisfy any chocoholic. In fact, being in the same room as these cakes would probably satisfy a chocolate craving!

MAKES 12 SLICES

- 300g chocolate (we used Galaxy, as it's a personal favourite, but feel free to choose whatever)
- 50g unsalted butter
- 50g runny honey
- 200g Crunchy Nut Clusters
- Pinch of ground cinnamon

I like this recipe, because you get to use a bain marie, which is my favourite cooking term to say: bain marie. It makes melting chocolate sound like a really posh cooking utensil, when it's just a pan and a bowl!

So, get your bain marie going and melt down your chocolate. While this is happening melt the butter in a separate pan and stir in the honey. Add the honey and butter liquid to the chocolate in the bain marie, stirring continuously until it has melted, then remove from the heat.

Line a 22cm square baking tin with greaseproof paper. This does involve multitasking as you're still stirring your chocolate in the bain marie. Place the Clusters in a large mixing bowl, and bash them with the end of a rolling pin or any other large blunt object you have lying around. If multitasking is not your forte, you can always do this first.

Add the cinnamon to the melted chocolate, give it a stir, and pour over the bashed clusters. Give the clusters a good mix, making sure they are completely covered in the chocolate, and pour into the lined baking tin. Spread out the mix evenly, then set aside to cool for about 30 minutes before putting it in the fridge to set. Maybe place on a windowsill, just like in the cartoons.

All that's left to do is turn it out from the tin, and cut it into your preferred shape. Go for squares, but if they end up as rhombuses no one will care, unless they've got OCD.

There's no better way to celebrate a friend's birthday, failing a job interview, or getting divorced, than with a showstopper of a cake. And I think this cake, with its twist on the classic Rice Krispie square, is worthy of a Great British Bake Off semi-final!

I've often found there are a lot of missed opportunities when it comes to celebrations; here are a few unheard-of days you should probably start celebrating, right away.

HALF BIRTHDAY
– it's basically a half-year celebration, so why not celebrate it?

CONCEPTION DAY
– exactly 9 months before your birthday, this was when your dad's seed was sown, and damn right it deserves a celebration.

REVERSE BIRTHDAY
– not everyone gets to celebrate this, so basically it's your birth date reversed; e.g. my birthday is on 10 May (10/5) so my reverse birthday is 5 November (5/10).

It can be tricky getting presents out of people, but if you offer up a cake, the presents will follow.

OK, each layer here needs to be made separately, so melt a large knob of butter (5g) and 35g marshmallows together in a pan with 1 teaspoon of food colouring. Make sure you get the good food colouring from the baking store, as the ones from the supermarkets are good but might not be as vibrant and will tone down the scale of the celebration – meaning less presents.

Add 40g Rice Krispies and mix well. Press the coloured cereal into a 22cm round cake tin with the back of a metal spoon. This can be quite messy as the marshmallow is very sticky and has the consistency of spider webs, so cover the mixture with baking paper before smoothing over the paper. Repeat this process with every colour of the rainbow. If you have only one cake tin you can keep the layers separate with pieces of baking paper. Make sure you keep the layers in the fridge as you make each one.

MAKES 1 BIG CAKE
- 35g unsalted butter
- 245g white marshmallows
- Several food colourings – red, orange, yellow, green, blue, indigo, violet
- 280g Rice Krispies

For the frosting
- 300g unsalted butter
- 1 x 454g or 2 x 213g tub marshmallow fluff
- 500g icing sugar
- Hundreds and thousands, to decorate

To make the frosting, beat the butter with an electric mixer until soft, then add the marshmallow fluff and beat further. Next, add half of the icing sugar and mix until smooth, then add the remaining icing sugar. Use a small amount of the icing to cement the layers together; remember to do them in the correct order according to the colours of the rainbow. That is not the rhyme: 'red and yellow and pink and green, purple and orange and blue, I can sing a rainbow, sing a rainbow, sing a rainbow, too', 'cause these are not the correct colours. This is one of the first things we learn in life which isn't true, and this is why we have trust issues! The correct order is: red, orange, yellow, green, blue, indigo, violet (Richard of York gave battle in vain).

Once you have built your cake, spread the frosting over the top and sides of the entire cake but leave some to add to your piping bag to finish off. If you need to smooth the frosting you can run a metal knife under very hot water, dry it with a cloth and use the back to smooth it down. Finish off by piping the remaining frosting around the corners and decorate with wee swirly bits. Scatter some hundreds and thousands, because once I presented this and was asked why I had made a mashed-potato cake!

RAINBOW POP CELEBRATION CAKE

ROSIE'S CRUNCHYNUT GRANOLA TARTS

This recipe has been cooked up by my good friend, Rosie Taylor. We were roommates in our mid-twenties and Rosie taught me everything I know about cooking. You might find it hard to believe, but most of my early twenties were spent avoiding the kitchen and pouring a bowl of cereal for most meals!

Rosie taught me the difference between whisking and beating, grilling and toasting, and in return I taught her how to poop standing up.

Rosie has always been a glamorous character, and has often been described as a drag queen trapped inside a woman's body. But if a woman can look glamorous while searching for her bra on a nightclub floor, then she's doing something right.

MAKES 12 SMALL OR ONE BIG ONE

- One 500g pack of shortcrust pastry
- 220g good-quality dark chocolate, finely chopped
- 80ml double cream
- 40g soft light brown sugar
- 40g unsalted butter, plus extra for greasing
- 250g Crunchy Nut Glorious Oat Granola, hazelnut and choc flavour, lightly crushed

OK, let's get the pastry on. Preheat the oven to 180°C and grease a 12-hole muffin tin.

Next, roll out the pastry to about 3mm thick, cut out twelve 10cm diameter circles and press them into the holes in the tin. Now you'll need to blind-bake them (just a fancy name for baking them with baking beans in, instead of the filling) by lining each hole with a little baking parchment and a few baking beans for 12 minutes. Remove the beans and paper and cook the pastry for a further 10 minutes until golden brown. Let the pastry cases cool while you make the filling.

Now it's time to get saucy, chocolate saucey. Put the chocolate into a heatproof bowl and put to one side. Pop your cream and sugar into a small pan and stir while bringing to the boil; once it starts to bubble, take it off the heat and pile in the chopped chocolate, stirring. After a few minutes, add the butter and stir everything to combine. Your mouth should be heavily salivating at this point.

Now let's get filling these bad boys. Mix the crushed granola and half of the chocolate sauce in a bowl until the oats are all covered. Divide the mixture evenly (or as evenly as possible) into the cooled bases, top up with the remaining chocolate sauce, then leave for an hour to set. Now enjoy with a good ol' brew. Bliss.

WHERE'S ALAN & GARY?

Camden Stables Market is always crowded, especially in the area around the Cereal Killer Café! Alan and Gary are somewhere in the crowd – can you spot them?

If you found the boys, maybe you can also try to spot a few others – The Spice Girls; the Honey Monster; Prince William with Kate and the kids; Timmy Mallett; Jon Snow and Daenerys from Game of Thrones with one of her dragons; Pamela Anderson and Boris Johnson.

CEREAL KILLER CAFE

ANSWERS

p42 - Magic Eyes

If you stare long enough you should be able to see a Froot Loop ring in the top left pattern; a sugar cube (or possibly a Rubik's Cube!), bottom left; a star, top right and, the most difficult one, the word CEREAL, bottom right.

p66 - Pop Cereal Quizzicle Answers

1. Melanie and Martina
2. 'Stars'
3. Posh Spice
4. Aztec, Industrial, Futuristic, Medieval
5. Sugar
6. Preston and Logan
7. Andrew Ridgeley and George Michael
8. 1988 (for UK viewers)
9. 4 delicious wholegrains
10. Phillip Schofield
11. Malibu and California are both correct
12. 'It's Alright'
13. 23
14. Byker Grove
15. 'Sad'
16. Blue
17. Mashed potato
18. 'Mr Blobby'
19. Beetlejuice-Beetlejuice-Beetlejuice
20. Tia and Tamera

p74 - Word Search

p90 - Mixed-Up Words

1. Chocopotomus
2. Fruit Loops
3. The Lion King
4. Snap Crackle and Pop
5. Chocolate milk
6. Cabbage Patch Kids
7. Shredded Wheat
8. Lucky Charms
9. Crunchy Nut Cornflakes
10. Kellogg's Ricicles

p82-83 - Spot the Difference

p126-127 - Where's Alan & Gary?

THANKS!

Alan, Gary and the publishers would like to thank Jamie Smart for his great cartoon versions of the twins; Ross Thompson for all his hard work on the 'Where's Alan & Gary?' scene and Steve Fearn and Kirsty Corcoran at Raisio/Halo Foods for their help with the Honey Monster feature.

We would also like to thank Rosie Taylor and Billy Rayner for their recipe contributions; all the staff at Cereal Killer Café for their help in tasting every recipe, good or bad; Charlotte Ridge and Adrian Sington for getting us the deal; Lizzy Gray, Anna Mrowiec, Rod Green, Marcus Scudamore, Martin Stiff and everyone who helped out on the book; Tony the Tiger for being a talking animal cartoon role model, and lastly our parents for birthing us and making this all possible.

And cake, we would like to thank cake.